THE SCANDALOUS GOSPEL OF JESUS

THE
SCANDALOUS
GOSPEL OF JESUS

*What's So Good About
the Good News?*

PETER J. GOMES

HarperOne
An Imprint of HarperCollins*Publishers*

HarperOne

HarperCollins books may be purchased for educational, business, or sales promotional use. For information please write: Special Markets Department, HarperCollins Publishers, 10 East 53rd Street, New York, NY 10022.

HarperCollins Web site: http://www.harpercollins.com
HarperCollins®, 🏭 ®, and HarperOne™
are trademarks of HarperCollins Publishers.

FIRST HARPERCOLLINS PAPERBACK EDITION PUBLISHED IN 2008

Designed by Joseph Rutt

Library of Congress Cataloging-in-Publication Data
is available upon request.

ISBN 978–0–06–000074–5

08 09 10 11 12   RRD (H)   10 9 8 7 6 5 4 3 2 1

To
Pelham Wilder Jr.
1920–
and
Sterly Lebey Wilder
1921–1998

Splendid partners
Wonderful friends

Contents

PART 3
Where Do We Go from Here?

Introduction

The great principle dominating the composition of Scripture is that of the ascent towards discovery.

—Henri Daniel-Rops,
What Is the Bible?

When I remember that the literal translation of the term *gospel* is "good news," I recall a wonderful encounter with her late Majesty Queen Elizabeth, the Queen Mother. In the summer of 2001, I found myself at divine service in the parish church in Windsor Great Park, where the royal family attends Sunday worship when in Windsor. The parish church is tiny, Victorian, and Gothic, complete with a choir composed of estate workers, and on the Sunday in question both Her Majesty Queen Elizabeth II and the Queen Mother were in attendance.

To my great delight, immediately following the service I was invited to join mother and daughter for drinks at Royal Lodge, the Windsor residence of the Queen Mother. Then in her one hundred and second year, she was holding court in the form of a splendid pre-luncheon party in a setting worthy of a Merchant and Ivory film, and eventually I was summoned into the royal presence, where Her Majesty maintained a lively conversation. Among other observations, the Queen Mother remarked on how excellent the sermon had been. "Don't you agree?" she asked me, which is a difficult question for an honest clergyman to answer, so I did what anyone would do under the circumstances: I agreed. Then, with that world-class twinkle in her eye, the Queen Mother remarked, "I do like a bit of good news on Sunday, don't you?"

To that declaration I gave hearty assent, for the great gift of the Christian faith is the proclamation of good news even in bad or difficult times. To be reminded of the good news is to be reminded of the real gospel, and in some sense I owe what follows here to that casually accurate remark of the Queen Mother, who unknowingly serves as the inspiration for these thoughts on the substance of Jesus' preaching and teaching. I cherish her remark as a reminder not only of a delightful and memorable morning, but of why Christians continue to be sustained by the real gospel message of Jesus Christ. For that small insight into a great truth I shall always be in happy debt to her late Majesty.

For many years now I have preached and taught from the Bible. As an ordained Christian minister I am expected to do so, and as a university preacher and professor I regard this task as one of my greatest and happiest responsibilities. It is not, however, easy work. The Bible itself is a complicated collection of books, written by many hands over many years and in a wide variety of media, including poetry, history, parable, theology, and apocalypse. To say that the books are inspired or written according to a theory of divine dictation does not make them any easier to read or understand. If the Bible were simple to understand and easy to appropriate, then preachers and theologians would have nothing to do and there could be no excuse for the spiritual and moral chaos in which the world habitually finds itself.

To some degree, one more book on the Bible is always justified, for if we honestly search the scriptures and live honestly in our own time and not in some other, we are likely to discover something new or hear something old afresh. We can appreciate the enigmatic truth in the title of one of Marcus Borg's most successful books of biblical scholarship, *Meeting Jesus Again for the First Time.*

So I venture one more book on the Bible, and presume to add to the groaning shelves on this seemingly inexhaustible subject. This, however, is a Bible book with a difference. When in 1996 I wrote *The Good Book: Reading the Bible with Mind and Heart,* I did so with the assumption that the most popular bestseller was not necessarily the best-read book, and I wanted the average person to be able to read the Bible with the benefit of a century of the best critical scholarship. My hope was that people would pass beyond their reverence for scripture and actually see what it had to say. In my second book in this series, *The Good Life: Truths That Last in Times of Need,* I hoped to make it possible for the faithful and intelligent reader of the Bible to apply it to that which helped make a good life, rather than just a good living. I wrote in the heated aftermath of the terrible events of September 11, 2001, with the hope that the Bible and the truths to which it points would issue in the living of lives of noble purpose.

Now I write another Bible book, with the radical suggestion that we use the Bible to go beyond the Bible and embrace that to which it points: the gospel, or the good news. In a time when it is easier to write about doom and gloom than about hope and promise, I suggest that Jesus came into the world not as a Bible teacher directing us back into a text, but as one who proclaimed a realm beyond the Bible. He proclaimed his good news against the conventional wisdom of his day, taking up with unacceptable people and advancing dangerous, even revolutionary, ideas, nearly all of which remain to be discovered and acted upon. I have always been persuaded of the truth of the aphorism attributed to G. K. Chesterton, that

"Christianity is not a faith that has been tried and found wanting, but a faith that has been wanted and never tried."

My argument, initially inspired by Vanderbilt University theologian Edward Farley's seminal article, entitled "Preaching the Bible and Preaching the Gospel,"[1] has taken me to the conviction that in order to take seriously the gospel, that is, the content and direction of Jesus' own preaching and teaching, we must dare to venture beyond the Bible itself and into the uncharted territory of the gospel. I was encouraged to do this by a sense that the times in which Jesus did his preaching and teaching were remarkably similar to our own. Then, as now, there was a large and lively enterprise of religion, but beneath the surface of conformity ran deep rivers of fear, disappointment, and frustration. Then, as now, the world found it easier to deal with bad news or conventional wisdom, and thus resisted the in-breaking of anything new or confrontational. Jesus' death on the cross made it clear that the world to which he preached the glad tidings was not prepared to hear them or to take seriously the one who proclaimed them.

The "battles for the Bible," which have been fought as skirmishes in the larger culture wars for centuries but with a particular intensity in our own times, have not proved edifying. There may be more Bibles in more tongues and hands now than at any other time in human history, yet the world seems no nearer to the kingdom of God than it ever has been. As a consequence of this view, some say that the gospel is a fraud, an illusion sustained only by a gullible public, and others say that things are so bad that the end of the world must be at hand, and the sooner it comes, the better.

I embrace neither of these positions in this book, and I write for those for whom neither position is credible or acceptable. I believe that there is a vast universe of people of goodwill and reasonable intelligence eager to give the Christian faith a chance to speak in their lives and world, who are not satisfied with the conventional wisdom, and who find things as they are simply not good enough. The overwhelming religiosity of the United States in the twenty-first century notwithstanding, with public Christianity nearly a social and political fashion statement and religious discourse saturating our culture at every turn, I continue to believe that we are living in needy, pagan times. Instead of inhabiting the time of one of America's periodic revivals of religion or "Great Awakenings," we live, I am convinced, in times more like those described in the biblical book of Judges: "In those days there was no king in Israel; all the people did what was right in their own eyes."[2]

I do not offer this book as a polemic, although I do from time to time take strong issue with the conventional wisdom of both the pious and the secular. I am not out to bash anyone, and I hope I can improve the quality of discourse among the many sincere people of goodwill who differ greatly in their views on faith in our times. I do worry that with so much religion about, and with the ever-increasing polarization of our convictions, sooner rather than later we will discover that the problem in our culture is not religion but the religious. It is my highest hope to appeal not so much to those who are already set in their convictions, but to that vast company of readers willing to investigate a point of view that may not be its own. Preaching to the converted and, depending on which one, the choir, is a waste of time, and I live in the hope of doing better than that. Should success or failure, or, alas, rank indifference, attend my efforts, I nonetheless rest content in the spiritual ambition of one of my favorite Protestants, Richard Baxter, a veteran of the religious wars of seventeenth-century England:

In necessary things, unity;
In doubtful things, liberty;
In all things, charity.

— I —

The Trouble
with Scripture

ONE

We Start with the Bible

In the new paradigm, what-is-preached shifts from the Bible or a passage of the Bible to Gospel and elements of the world of Gospel.

—Edward Farley,
Practicing Gospel

Some years ago I was on a night flight from Boston to London on a Saturday and was to preach in a London church on Sunday morning; in those days I was not intimidated by jet lag and looked forward to my engagement within a few hours of landing at Heathrow Airport. Then, midway over the Atlantic Ocean we encountered significant turbulence and were warned to keep our seatbelts fastened. Less concerned about the storm than about my sermon, I took out my notes and my Bible, and as I read, the lady beside me, who had been mercifully quiet throughout the flight, observed me. As the turbulence increased she noticed that I was reading the Bible, and finally she asked, nervously, "Do you know something that I should know?"

In the preaching profession that is known as an "illustration in search of a sermon"—although it was one I declined to preach at that moment. As with so many people, my seatmate had assumed that the answer to the present dilemma, whatever it was, would be found in the Bible; and while she might not know where or how to look for it, she assumed that, as a clergyman, I did. To many people the Bible remains a book of magical properties: taking an oath or swearing on a stack of Bibles is meant to assure the truth, for example, and a Bible in the drawer of a hotel bedside table implies not only the presence of the Gideons but a formula for relief in moments of temptation or desolation.

We assume that the Bible has something to tell us that we need to hear. It is read out faithfully in every church in the world; preachers protest that they preach from the Bible and only the Bible, and Bible schools, Bible colleges, and Bible institutes have never been more popular. To turn on cable television is to discover a wide variety of Bible preachers and teachers, from well-known televangelists to any media-savvy preacher who can afford a satellite disk or a website. The camera angles always show large auditoriums filled with enthusiastic listeners, their Bibles open to follow the exposition of the text, and many of the programs have their own patented Bible courses of study which, for an appropriate contribution, are available for purchase.

No one in the Bible business simply says, "Read the text and it will be made plain to you." Although many will argue for the "plain sense" of scripture, that sense is made clear only through the guidance of one who presumably knows more about it than we do; and there is the assumption that once we read and understand it, the Bible will have something useful to say to us. This confidence in the text's ability to speak to our condition reminds me of the practice of settling disputes and troubles by opening the Bible at random and putting one's finger on a verse, which is taken to be the answer to the problem. Had I applied that principle to the question of my seatmate on my flight to London, what would she or I have made of the situation if my finger had landed, for example, on John 6:12, which reads in part: "Gather up the fragments left over, that nothing may be lost"?[1]

We start with the Bible because, like Everest, it is there, and it looms large. There is no point in pretending otherwise, but while we may begin there, are we meant to end up there as well? If it is a means, to what is it a means? I suggest that the Bible, in all its complex splendor, is but the means to a greater end, which is the good news, the glad tidings, the gospel. Jesus came preaching—we are told this in all the Gospels—but nowhere in the Gospels is there a *true* claim that he came preaching the New Testament, or even Christianity. It still shocks some Christians to realize that Jesus was not a Christian, that he did not know "our" Bible, and that what he preached was substantially at odds with his biblical culture, and with ours as well.

A Matter of Interpretation

There is the doubtlessly apocryphal story of the accountant in a large firm who handled a deceptively simple question put by his boss, "What is two times two?" by replying, "What would you like it to be, sir?" and thereby landed a plum job. To many people the notion of interpretation, particularly where the Bible is concerned, seems much akin to that of our wily accountant, for interpretation is somehow seen as an alien and intervening force between the reader and the truth of the text.

For many years I have taught a course in Harvard College, "The Christian Bible and Its Interpretation," and at the conclusion of the introductory lecture I invite questions from the hundreds of opening-day "shopping" students who might under the right circumstances decide to take the course. Invariably someone asks, "Is this a course about what the Bible says, or is it a course about what people say the Bible says?" It is a hostile question, and I don't make the situation any easier when I say that the very act of reading is an act of interpretation, and that in a course of this sort it is impossible not to read what people are both finding in the text and bringing to it. One does not have to be a postdoctoral student in literary criticism to know that a sixteenth-century German Lutheran and a twenty-first-century Latin American Catholic are likely to read and interpret scripture differently. My course is a survey of how readings of the same constant text have varied over the centuries, from the formation of the canon to our present time, dependent on context and subtext. A community in exile will read differently from a community in apparent full possession of all it surveys, with those who have nothing welcoming the promised overturning of the standing order, and those who have much of this world's goods not longing for the end of the age.

Depending, then, upon how one reads and interprets, either the Bible is a textbook for the status quo, a book of quiescent pieties and promises, or it is a recipe for social change and transformation. There are churches dedicated to each point of view, each claiming its share of the good news; but what is good news for some is often bad news for somebody else. We will see how this double-edged sword of the gospel makes Jesus' own preaching and teaching so dangerous, not only way back then but right here and now, and we will see why it is a very dangerous thing to take seriously the question "What would Jesus do?"

Ignorance and Reticence

A decade ago when I wrote *The Good Book: Reading the Bible with Mind and Heart*, I hoped that I would contribute a small bit to the raisir̲̲̲ ̲̲̲lical literacy in a country and culture that increasingly pride̲̲̲ ̲̲̲ on its biblical bona fides. After all, Jimmy Carter described ̲̲̲ ̲̲̲nself as a born-again Christian and taught Sunday school, ̲̲̲onald Reagan relished biblical imagery and endeared himself to religious conservatives, Bill Clinton could quote scripture with the best, and now George W. Bush is perhaps our most publicly professed chief executive in the history of the presidency. It seemed to me to be imperative that we know more about what could and could not be said about the Bible as more and more of our public policy decisions seemed to be based upon vague appeals to biblical authority.

In *The Good Book* I made no pretensions to new or earth-shattering scholarship. As noted by one of my mildly censorious colleagues on the Harvard Divinity School faculty, I had simply put down what any seminarian ought to know after the first year of study. What amazed me, therefore, in my many travels across the country to book fairs, church halls, and media interviews was how new and unfamiliar this material seemed to so many. It was as if the past five hundred years of biblical scholarship had not existed, as if we were dealing with a book as preciously obscure to the average reader as Jerome's Latin Vulgate.

This should not have come as such a surprise, however, for when I had gone off to Bates College more than forty years earlier, I had been warned by my pious old Sunday school teacher, for whom I had memorized vast quantities of the King James Bible, "Don't take a Bible course; they'll give you criticism and you'll lose Christ!" "Bible 101," a staple in every required liberal arts curriculum in those days, did introduce us to a more complicated biblical universe than the one that most of us had left behind in Sunday school. I had never noticed, for example, that there were two creation stories, that the second version was older than the first, and that Moses could hardly have written the first five books except posthumously.

Instead of determining the moral authority of scripture and dealing with the truth-claims of the resurrection, Bible 101 was more concerned with textual criticism, authorship, historicity, and the formation of the canon. English majors had a special course in the Bible so that they could make sense of biblical allusions in Shakespeare, Milton, and T. S. Eliot.

For many people, certified as well educated by the possession of a bachelor's degree, this would be the first and last exercise in anything like formal biblical studies. For the rest of their days, if they were religiously inclined, they would depend upon devotional biblical bits, unedifying preaching from the Bible, and the therapy that passes for "Bible study" in most Protestant churches.

I, however, did not know when to quit and went on to divinity school. At Harvard in those days we had the benefit of the teachers of our teachers, for our biblical professors, including Krister Stendahl, George Ernest Wright, Frank Moore Cross, Jr., Helmut Koester, and Amos N. Wilder, were the men who wrote the books that everybody else used. We were schooled in the fine arts of textual exegesis, the history of criticism, the close study of particular books, and the debates about authorship. Barth, Bultmann, and Tillich were as relevant to our biblical studies as were Matthew, Mark, Luke, and John, and we were even persuaded against our natural desires that study in the original languages, however mediocre, was superior to English-only biblical study. In the introduction to the New Testament, our class was divided into the "Greeks," who actually read the Koine text, and the "Barbarians," who could not.

Also in those days, Harvard was not unique in its emphasis on biblical study in all its complexity. Nearly every seminary was devoted to this course of study, and it was noteworthy that the conservative theological schools were even more devoted to thorough biblical study, but with the agenda of maintaining biblical orthodoxy.

When I visit old colleagues and students I always look in their bookcases, and I usually find that those books having pride of place but showing very little wear and tear are the books of biblical scholarship. This perhaps explains the phenomenon of the reticent pulpit, for how else can one account for the remarkable lack of biblical knowledge that exists in the pews except for the reticence of the pulpit? Recently I asked some of my students in the ministry if their biblical studies had any effect on their preaching, and most said that they found it next to impossible to translate what they knew of biblical criticism into the vernacular of their preaching. When they tried to do so, people complained. When they offered to Bible classes the benefits of their knowledge, they were told that people preferred the way they had always done things; and this remains the case. In his sermon "Shall the Fundamentalists Win?" Harry Emerson Fosdick famously said, "... people don't care about the Jebusites, etc."

If to this state of affairs one adds the iconography of most Protestant churches, which gives pride of place to an open Bible propped up between flowers or candlesticks, and the declaration that "This is the word of the Lord," then we have given the Bible a position that does not permit of criticism or examination. In those circumstances the reticence of the pulpit is understandable, but the result is costly, for an ignorant people and a reticent pulpit are the recipe for theological and biblical disaster.

A Greater Problem Than This

The inadequate study of the Bible is bad, and I was once naïve enough to think that if we could only improve our methods of instruction and proclamation, then we would be well on the way to a more informed reading and living of scripture. There are places where rigorous Bible study is the rule and not the exception, but what does it profit a congregation or a believer to have mastered all the critical skills of biblical study, to know all there is to know about the Gospels, but nothing about the gospel itself?

My predecessor as Plummer Professor of Christian Morals in The Memorial Church at Harvard University, George Arthur Buttrick, was generally regarded as one of the princes of the pulpit in his generation. He was quoted by everyone, and perhaps most famously endeared himself to generations of preachers through his editorship of *The Interpreter's Bible*, which has brought many a preacher from Saturday night to Sunday morning. Buttrick, however, was not only a great preacher but a great teacher of preachers. He would listen to the student sermons in his course, comment on the structure, the gestures, the biblical analysis, the exposition of the text, and invariably would ask, in his quavering voice, "But, Mr. Jones, where's the good news? Where's the good news?"

By this question George Buttrick did not mean what many contemporary preachers seem to assume, which is that every sermon must end on a happy, upbeat note like the fourth movement of a classical symphony. No; Buttrick understood that the sermon in general and the text of the Bible in particular had to be measured against a more exacting standard than its own words, and that standard was the gospel. Where is the good news in the oft-repeated story of the Prodigal Son? Where is the good news of the road to Emmaus? Where is the good news of the Seven Last Words from the Cross? Where is the good news in the book of Revelation?

Buttrick understood what we must now recover: that what we call "the Bible" is only the means to a deepened understanding of what Jesus called the gospel, or glad tidings, and that for us to understand this we have to understand afresh, or perhaps for the first time, the radical nature of the substance of Jesus' preaching.

Early on in their theological studies, seminarians learn that Jesus, who came preaching, became the preached. It is adequate but not sufficient to say that Jesus is the gospel or the good news. That is true, but it is not all there is to the matter. Those who heard Jesus preaching and teaching heard him give specific utterance to a point of view that he himself called the glad tidings. He came preaching not himself but something to which he himself pointed, and in our zeal to crown him as the content of our preaching, most of us have failed to give due deference to the content of his preaching.

It is easy to see why. In the first case, what Jesus proclaimed did not happen, nor has it yet; the glad tidings remain a proclamation of things to come. The world remains pretty much as it was when he preached his first sermon at Nazareth, and although there are many more Christians now, and the world is older, that *Yum Yahweh*—day of the Lord—appears no nearer now than it was at the time of Jesus' proclamation.

So, one of the reasons it is easy to ignore the content of Jesus' preaching is that it is not confirmed by the experience of history. That, for example, is why Advent is a more painful season than Lent. In Lent we can apply piety to personal circumstance, we can recreate something of an affinity with the historical phenomenon of Christ's suffering and of our own development through suffering. Advent, on the other hand, speaks of a perennial hope, a great expectation that, despite the language of the hymns that tell us that the day is drawing near and that light prevails over darkness, actually seems just like the "same old, same old." How many "theologies of hope" can trump the stubborn facts of good news postponed?

If we read the Epistles, especially those of Saint Paul within the circle of the writer's expectations and those of his first audience, we can only be disappointed in our expectations. The very first book of the New Testament canon, not Matthew, which has canonical priority, but 1 Thessalonians, which is older, is concerned with the anxieties of the faithful about the realization of the good news. The writer, especially in 1 Thessalonians 4, reassures the faithful that they should not lose heart even though many have already died. In chapter 5, the writer offers his famous analogy of the Lord coming like "a thief in the night," or "a woman in travail." The word is to wait, work, and watch, and not to lose heart or patience. Modern audiences find solid comfort in these counsels; the only alternative is to proclaim an imminent return of the Lord, an end of the edge. There is a large and vibrant culture of expectation that suggests that the time is near.

In the meantime we can understand a reluctance to focus too much on the content of Jesus' preaching, largely because it is easier to talk about him than it is to talk about what he talked about.

Changing the Focus

The radical nature of the Jesus story is not in the way of his death—the *via dolorosa*—nor is it even in his glorious resurrection, to which we instinctively respond when strangers fill the churches on Easter. The radical dimension of the Jesus story has to do with the content of his preaching, the nature of the glad tidings that he announced to be at hand. It would take a miracle and a man of Mel Gibson's genius and chutzpah to make a film about what biblical writer Thomas D. Hanks calls the subversive gospel. This is the good news that was bad news to many in Jesus' time, so much so that at the beginning of his preaching they nearly killed him, and at the end of his ministry they succeeded.

There is a famous *New Yorker* cartoon that shows plutocrats leaving a church after having said sweet nothings to the preacher at the door. In the caption the wife, swathed in furs and jewels, says to her top-hatted husband, "It can't be easy for him not to offend us." In the wildly popular British import comedy *The Vicar of Dibley*, the vicar, the bodacious Geraldine Granger, is often accused by her Tory-blue Senior Warden of preaching "socialist twaddle." "Why not stick to the gospel?" he asks; and she sweetly replies that "this *is* the gospel."

If the focus is nearly always on the man for others who in the short term loses but who one of these days will return in triumph to win, then it is no wonder that so much of the Christian faith is either obsessed by the past or seduced by the prospects of a glorious future. In the meantime, things continue in their bad old way, and we live as realists in a world in which reality is nearly always the worst-case scenario.

The last thing the faithful wish for is to be disturbed. Thus it is easy to favor the Bible over the gospel, because the gospel can somehow be seen as those nice, even compelling, stories about Jesus that have next to nothing to do with us "until he comes."

In my preaching course I assign texts to my students for Sunday preaching. They don't like it, for they would rather choose their own texts or preach their tradition's lectionary, and I understand that. I choose contentious texts, however, passages with which they would never willingly wrestle, and often I choose from the Gospels some of the eschatological stories having to do with justice and the reversal of fortune. One of my favorites is the story of rich man Dives and the poor beggar Lazarus, the terrifying account of the rich man who on earth enjoys good things but in death ends up in hell while Lazarus, the beggar at his gates, ends up in Abraham's bosom. The rich man, even in hell, is accustomed to being listened to and so he asks that Lazarus direct some water to relieve his parched lips. It is not to be. He then asks for his brothers still on earth to be warned to do good and not to follow his example so that they may avoid his fate. Father Abraham declines, however, saying that they have had Moses and the prophets and every opportunity to repent. It is now too late.

My students find this story relatively easy to exegete, but nearly impossible to preach. "Why?" I ask. "Our people wouldn't stand for it," they reply; or "It is not motivational enough"; or "I don't believe God behaves that way." When I suggest that apparently Jesus took the story seriously enough to tell it, and that the evangelists took it seriously enough to record it and ascribe it to Jesus, their best response is, "Well, that was then and this is now." Is there a good word here? Is this a part of the good news? How does this square with so much of the rest of Jesus' preaching and teaching? I think we know the answer. The gospel can easily be lost in the Bible. It was not so with Jesus, for he found the Hebrew Bible—the only one he knew—the means to the gospel. If we look carefully at what constituted his preaching, his definition of gospel, we might be surprised to find how much the gospel is at odds with conventional Christianity. It is very difficult to preach the gospel as Jesus did without giving offense, and the world has been filled with people perfectly capable of being offended.

It is not that we are ignorant. We know what gives offense, which is probably why we spend so much time talking about sex and Jesus spent so much time talking about money. When the emperor Constantine ceased to prosecute the Christians and made toleration of their religion Roman policy, he knew that the way to domesticate the incipient rival to his own ultimate power was to make the church comfortable and complacent; and that to do this, the radical edge of Jesus' preaching and teaching of the gospel would have to be dulled. The church, then, is made an agency of continuity rather than of change, conformity rather than transformation becomes the reigning ideology of the day, and the church that is comfortable with the powers-that-be is no threat to them.

The earliest translators of the Bible into vernacular English, William Tyndale and John Wycliffe, were held as dangerous and put to death as heretics because they argued that if people could read the gospel for themselves and see what Jesus said and did, and compared that biblical gospel conduct with the behavior of the bishops, priests, and deacons who presumed to preach in his name to an ignorant population, then there would be the basis of a social revolution. The *Magnificat*'s proud boast that "He hath filled the poor with good things, and the rich he hath sent empty away" would proclaim that the status quo is not the gospel's work but the work of clever and self-interested persons. Those shrewd bishops and officers of state recognized that in those translations of the Bible into English was to be found a threat to everything they valued; and they were determined not to be threatened.

When Martin Luther King Jr. was urged by the respectable Christian clergy of Birmingham, Alabama, to stop his protests on the grounds that good people would be intimidated, even turned off, by tactics that, the white clergy argued, were essentially un-Christian, King replied:

> In your statement you asserted that our actions, even though peaceful, must be condemned because they precipitate violence. Isn't this like condemning the robbed man because his possession of money precipitated the evil act of robbery?... Isn't this like condemning Jesus because his unique God-consciousness and never-ceasing devotion to God's will precipitated the evil act of the Crucifixion?

From ancient times onward, every movement for social justice has been charged with misunderstanding Jesus' true intentions. Martin Luther, the Father of the Reformation, was horrified when German peasants took as the basis for their revolt against the established order what he had given them in the Reformation Bible; and when in eighteenth-century England and nineteenth-century North America Christians argued against chattel slavery on the grounds that it was an offense to the gospel, they were sharply criticized by those who regarded themselves as good biblical Christians. In the twentieth century, first with the appeal of the gospel resulting in the so-called theologies of liberation in the most oppressed places on earth, and subsequently in the battles for a change in attitude and policy toward sexual minorities, those in favor of these changes always have the gospel on their side but are routinely repulsed by those who argue from the Bible.

No One to Blame but Us

For the parlous state of affairs in which we find ourselves, the church has no one to blame but itself. The new pope, Benedict XVI, decried the secular culture in his sermon to the College of Cardinals, speaking eloquently and passionately against a culture of arrogance and self, the "dictatorship of relativity." It is this very same pope, however, who as Joseph Cardinal Ratzinger declared the theologies of liberation—which for a short time flourished in the churches of Latin America and Africa—as without God, and equated them with communism. Nearly all of his predecessors on the throne of Peter were faced with the nonresolvable conundrum of doctrine that argues for the status quo versus the radical words of Jesus, whose gospel would not have been unsympathetic to the famous social slogan of the nineteenth century, "From each according to his ability, to each according to his need."

Rarely has the Christian church risked its temporal position to proclaim the glad tidings of Jesus' preaching and teaching, for the risk to the status quo is almost always too great. The danger of the gospel is that if we take it seriously, then like Jesus we will risk all, and might even lose all. On the other hand, we do not know the names of those guards who executed Dietrich Bonhoeffer in Germany at the end of World War II, but Bonhoeffer's name and, more important, his example, live through all time. Could it be that we spend so much time trying to make sense of the Bible, or making it conform to our set of social expectations, that we have failed to take to heart the essential content of the preaching and teaching of Jesus? When they stand to give their first sermon, all student preachers are reminded, "Remember, you are to preach the gospel, and not the Bible." Perhaps now, and in the pages that follow, is the time and place to look at just what Jesus preached and taught. How did it go down with his listeners? Is it any easier for us to hear than it was for them? If by this exercise we learn nothing else, we will discover that Jesus was always more concerned about tomorrow than about yesterday, but tomorrow's implications are lived out today, here and now. If we are sincere in wanting to know what Jesus would do, we must risk the courage to ask what he says, what he asks, and what he demands. Only if we do so will we be able to move, however cautiously and imperfectly, from the Bible to the gospel.

TWO

An Offending Gospel

And blessed is he who takes no offense at me.

—Matthew 11:6, RSV

If we want to know of a preacher who easily offends, one with whom it is easy to take umbrage, we have to look no farther than to John the Baptist, a fierce, wild prophet clad in animal skins, eating locusts and wild honey, and requiring the repentance of the sinful. Our first encounter with this radical cousin of Jesus is in Matthew 3, where he is described as preaching in the wilderness of Judea. Matthew tells us that John is the one who was spoken of by the prophet Isaiah when he said, "The voice of one crying in the wilderness: prepare ye the way of the Lord, make his paths straight."[1] John's preaching was effective: Jerusalem and all Judea went out to hear him, and all were baptized.

John was not, however, the most diplomatic of evangelists, for when he saw many members of the so-called establishment coming his way for baptism—the Pharisees and Sadducees and other good and respectable people—he called them a "brood of vipers" and told them that God could easily dispense with their services. For John, repentance was not merely social or an insurance policy against the dreadful day, but a sign that the dreadful day was very near. Now was the time of judgment, and the persons whose deeds reflected their repentance, and change of attitude and actions, would be spared, whereas those who outwardly turned but inwardly remained the same would not be spared. Here there was no inherited virtue, there were no spiritual aristocrats; everyone was subject to the judgment. John the Baptist's preaching made clear that those who thought themselves good in their own eyes, or seemed to be good in the eyes of others, were as needy of genuine repentance as the most notorious sinner, and perhaps even more so because they claimed the sanctity of an outward conformity to God's laws. John took nothing and no one for granted, and when he heard that Jesus was out preaching, he wanted to make certain that Jesus was the real article, the one who had been promised and not just another purveyor of spiritual charms.

Jesus came to John to be baptized, and although John might have declined to baptize Jesus on the grounds that Jesus should baptize him, he consented, and the baptism of Jesus occurs at the hands of John. Later on, John will want to make certain that Jesus is the one who will continue to proclaim the offending gospel, when from his prison cell, John asks about the deeds of Jesus and through his disciples asks Jesus some pointed questions, including, "Are you he who is to come, or shall we look for another?"[2] The implication is clear: should we invest our lives in you, or are you wasting our time? It is this question that Jesus answers in this way:

The blind receive their sight and the lame walk, lepers are cleansed and the deaf hear, and the dead are raised up, and the poor have good news preached to them. And blessed is he who takes no offense at me.[3]

Jesus answers in tangible terms, and the extraordinary has now become the routine. The usual order of things has been reversed. Transformation and renewal are signs of the age and time: if you want to know who I am, see what I do. This is not just an advertisement for the age of miracles; these miracles, or wonders, testify to the power of Jesus and are signs of the new age.

In the old age the blind were blind and thought to be so because of some sin that they or their parents had committed, and in the new age the blind are among the first to be given real vision. What is more radical than the first vision of one previously without sight? Everything, even the most mundane, is new. The same is true of the lame, whose affliction was also thought to be a cost of somebody's sin, and whose worst affliction was that they were dependent on others to help them get around. Think of the radical sense of independence given when the lame man in the Bible, confined to his litter, can obey the commandment of Jesus to "Take up thy bed, and walk." The formerly lame enters into a new world. In the "real" world the dead remain dead and there is nothing more certain than that, but in this new world of the gospel the dead, as Paul later puts it, "become the first fruits of them that sleep." To be dead is to have lost all chance and hope; to be given new life, a second chance, is to participate in the new creation at the most fundamental level, for if the dead can be revived, then the greatest fear there is—the fear of death—is itself destroyed. Later, Paul will say that the last enemy to be destroyed is death. Jesus, as proof of the legitimacy of his ministry and at its very start, proclaims that new life, the ultimate revival, is the most authoritative sign that something new and profoundly different is breaking in.

Some years ago, when I preached on this text I was upbraided by one of our most liberal and socially active listeners. She grabbed me by the lapels of my gown at the church door following the morning service, and told me how annoyed she was by that condescending lesson from which I preached my sermon. She noted that the blind received sight, the lame were healed, and presumably other afflictions were dealt with, but that the "structurally disincluded," by which expression I took her to mean the poor, were only preached at. "Typical," she said; "typical!" I was meant to be properly chastised, and I asked her why she assumed that the "poor" always referred to those who had less than herself. This was not an exercise in economics, at least not yet, but rather the promise that those who have nothing but bad news in their lives would have first claim upon the proclamation of good news. The content of good news was that in the future, in God's future, "soon and very soon," as the old gospel song puts it, that which was empty would be full and that which was on the bottom would be on top. When you have lost all help and hope, then to hear the glad tidings, to have the good news sent your way, is no small thing. It is a form of revival, of resurrection, and it ranks with the restoration of sight to the blind and mobility to the lame. It is a promise of things to come.

Jesus responds to John's question with these proofs of who he is and what he does, not so much to trump John as one rival would trump another, but to confirm John in his own ministry and expectations. These are extraordinary claims and doings, and so startling that somebody is bound to take offense. Jesus says, "Blessed"—or happy—is the person who, having heard all of this that is and is to come, will take no offense with the one who proclaims these truths and performs these deeds. The price of this proclamation, as we shall soon see, is very great.

Good News and Bad News

On the Sunday following the November 2004 presidential election, the one in which George W. Bush was declared elected by the press's newly discovered "values voter," I was preaching in an Episcopal church in California. It began as a sermon from the lectionary, pure and simple, but, as we discover to our cost, there is nothing pure and simple about the gospel. The so-called red states had triumphed over the so-called blue states, and as a native-born son of the Commonwealth of Massachusetts, I suppose no one could be truer blue than I. When I arrived at the church I was warned that many parishioners felt themselves to be islands of blue in a sea of red, but I was not intending to venture into politics and I resolved to preach on the gospel lectionary appointed for the day and heard by Episcopalians throughout North America on this All Saints Sunday.

The appointed gospel came from Luke 6:20–26, in a less familiar version of the Beatitudes that are better known in Matthew's Sermon on the Mount. The lesson starts out well enough:

> Jesus looked at his disciples and said,
> "Happy are you poor; the kingdom of God is yours.
> Happy are you who are hungry now; you will be filled.
> Happy are you who weep now; you will laugh."

The usual haze of familiarity covered the faces of those in church who were used to hearing the same verses over and over, to the extent that they sound like the scriptural equivalent of white sound or ambient noise. As the lesson went on, however, people began to sit up and take notice:

> "But how terrible for you who are rich now; you have had your
>   easy life;
> How terrible for you who are full now; you will go hungry!
> How terrible for you who laugh now; you will mourn and weep!
> How terrible when all men speak well of you, because their an-
>   cestors
> said the very same things to the false prophets."

An old Sunday school teacher of mine used to refer to these as the Woebetudes, because in the King James translation each bit of bad news begins with the word *woe*.

The sermon was not hard to preach, in the sense that the meaning of the text is quite clear. Those who appear to win by worldly standards, who are now the haves and not the have-nots, have every reason to be anxious about tomorrow, for if the good news, the gospel, is that worldly victories are only temporary and subject to reversal, then those who win today will lose tomorrow. Those who have it made today will have it unmade tomorrow. If you are at this moment at ease and satisfied, enjoy it, for it will not last; now is your reward, but now is not forever.

This was a message intended for people not used to winning, for whom tomorrow would always be better than today. The good news was for those who had no good news: healing for the sick, liberation for the captives, strength for the weak, and justice for the deprived. It was, in short, a reversal of fortune, and those who were on top would be cast down, while those who were downtrodden would be lifted up. This clearly was a message for those whose worldly circumstances stood in need of improvement, a word of encouragement to those mightily discouraged; and a crude, streetwise translation of this passage from Luke might sound like this: "You'll get yours, and I'll get mine." This does not mean that we will all share and share alike; it means that those of us who have much now will lose it, and those who have nothing will have more. It is the ultimate redistribution of wealth, and one can see why a certain kind of socialist would find it appealing, and a certain kind of capitalist find it appalling.

The gospel message in Luke is simply that knowing this, we now have a chance to do something about it before it is too late. Thus, in the verses that follow in Luke 6, Jesus tells us to love our enemies, practice the Golden Rule, love those beyond our comfort zone, and be merciful to others as we hope God will be merciful to us.

I fear that the niceties of this bit of exegesis were lost on a congregation filled with partisans, for the Republicans thought I was trashing their recent victory in general and George Bush in particular, and complained to the rector that I had "brought politics into the pulpit." The Democrats were delighted by the prospect of a biblically mandated reversal of fortune and felt that I had come to comfort them. Both were wrong. I preached simply what the gospel presented and, alas, situational listening did the rest. The incident reminded me of the exchange between Harry Truman and a supporter in the 1948 election. "Give 'em hell, Harry," was the slogan, to which Truman had replied, "I don't 'give 'em hell'; I tell the truth and it sounds like hell."

Good news to some will almost inevitably be bad news to others. In order that the gospel in the New Testament might be made as palatable as possible to as many people as possible, its rough edges have been shorn off and the radical edge of Jesus' preaching has been replaced by a respectable middle, of which "niceness" is now God. When Jesus came preaching, it was to proclaim the end of things as they are and the breaking in of things that are to be: the status quo is not to be criticized; it is to be destroyed. There is no appeal to an earlier Golden Age when things were done right, and the contemporary scene holds no promise, for it merely makes sacred the experiences of the people in power. The gospel's arena is the future, the time that is not yet and is to be, and thus everything short of that time is suspect, mortal, and inadequate.

I could see why my conservative friends might take umbrage with my sermon, although the umbrage would have been better taken with the gospel rather than with the preacher. Most of them, nearly all of the parish on either side of the political spectrum, were comfortable by the standards of this world, for what could be nicer than a nice life in California? If what they now enjoyed was to be taken away and given to those whom they had bested in the cultural wars, what point was there in going to church in the first place? If religion did not serve to confirm one's most basic instincts and secure one's hard-won gains, then what good was it?

Most people do not go to church to be confronted with the gap between what they believe and practice and what their faith teaches and requires. One of the reasons that religious people are often cultural conservatives, and that cultural conservatives take comfort in religion, is that religion is seen to confirm the status quo. When a member of a congregation says to the preacher at the door of a church on a Sunday, "That was a first-rate sermon," he or she is saying that the preacher said all the things with which the person agreed, but only half as well. In my own congregation I once asked an old sermon-taster—that is, a self-confessed connoisseur of preaching—how he would define a good sermon. "Why, one with which I agree," he answered. I admired his candor and dared not ask how many times I had preached a bad sermon, one contrary to his views.

In warning my preaching students of this dilemma, that people crave confirmation rather than confrontation in preaching, I remind them of how badly Jesus' first sermon went.

The Temptations

It's all in Luke 4, that first sermon in Jesus' home synagogue that started so well and ended so badly. For Christians, the Lenten season usually begins with an account of Jesus' forty days of temptation by Satan in the wilderness, and it is with this account that the fourth chapter of Luke opens. The temptation itself is not an easy thing to comprehend, since it comes upon Jesus immediately after his baptism and at the instigation of the Spirit. Many think of baptism as an inoculation against Satan and the tempting works of the devil, and with a sense of magic and invulnerability such that the combination of baptism and the power of the Holy Spirit will spare the believer the trials and tribulations of a fallen world. Thus it is useful to note that the first thing that happens to Jesus after his baptism is a season of intense temptation in the wilderness by Satan himself, as if the Spirit conspires in this form of spiritual hazing. Because of this particular juxtaposition of events in Jesus' life, it should be remembered that Satan finds a baptized believer a much worthier prize to capture than just any old soul.

Although readers believe that we know how the episode ends, it is unwise to underestimate the power and sophistication of Satan. It is not for nothing that in ancient Christian culture another name for Satan was the Old Deluder, and it is said that his most successful delusion to date is that he persuades very smart people that he doesn't exist. Here, in the account of Jesus' temptation, the reality of Satan is as much a given as the reality of Jesus; it is not "Savior" and "spook" here but two adversaries, and there is no assumption that Jesus will emerge unscathed from the encounter.

Why? The terror of the temptations put to Jesus is that they are so reasonable. In their own way they make sense, and what would be wrong in yielding to them? The temptations point out the fact that Satan usually appeals to us at the point where we feel ourselves spiritually strong, for where we think we are strong is not the place in which we invest our defensive energies. We think that Satan will attack us where we are weak, as if Satan is as rational as we are, but the proof of Satan's cleverness is that he appeals to those points where, more often than not, we feel secure.

All that Satan asks of Jesus in the wilderness is proof, evidence that Jesus is who he says he is. All Satan seems to want is evidence that God and Jesus are on the same side. Satan wants to be satisfied that Jesus and God are real and not mere figments of the spiritual imagination or a "bit of undigested beef," as Dickens has Scrooge say in the face of the ghostly apparitions that haunt him on Christmas Eve.

In the first case, appealing to Jesus' hunger after his extended fast, Satan invites him to satisfy that hunger and prove the power of his faith in God by commanding that the stones become bread. What could possibly be wrong with a little display of useful power? Jesus responds with a quotable verse of scripture about not living by bread alone.

The second temptation would make the gospel more efficient. Satan offers Jesus the world: "To you I will give all this authority and their glory; for it has been delivered to me and I give it to whom I will. If you then will worship me, it shall all be yours."[4] What an offer! With one gesture, the need for preaching, conversions, martyrdoms, missionaries, the whole enterprise, would be obviated and the world literally at Jesus' feet. This is perhaps the most dangerous and familiar of the three temptations, for who does not wish for absolute power, especially for the performance of absolute good? There is something very appealing in this promise of a new world order, a world delivered into the hands of its savior. Every leader worthy of his own ambitions and dreams lusts for the power to do without hindrance that which in his own estimation is good; and to achieve that without loss of life, conquest, prevarication, or duplicity is something for which every reformer yearns.

All Jesus had to do was to concede that the world was Satan's to give, for there was little evidence to the contrary, and then he could proceed with his own work, a work made simpler and easier by Satan's endorsement. Jesus declines, because to worship Satan would be to violate the commandment of Moses about having no gods other than God.

Of the three temptations the second is perhaps the most inge-
nious, the most devilish, as it were, for it proposes a choice between
a virtuous end, the Lordship of Christ over the world, and a less
than virtuous means, that of selling out to Satan. It also reminds us
that most of the world's enormous evils have resulted from the pursuit of some notion of good. Many modestly virtuous people have
committed deeds of outrageous evil in pursuit of an inadequate
definition of good, with each villain of history probably thinking of
himself as up to ultimate good. Both omelets and destiny, however,
require a few broken eggs. The landscape of human history is lit-
tered with the debris of ideals sacrificed to the idol of the ideal, and
this existential evidence, from the corruption of ancient kings to the
unsavory influence of contemporary fundamentalist fanatics, suggests that Satan may have been more than half right, for the world
does appear to belong to him.

Jesus, however, remembered that the world belongs to God, and
he would not compromise on that point in order to deliver to God
what was already God's. This is Satan's best shot, and he misses.

The third temptation is really very clever, for here Jesus is asked
to translate truth into action. The third temptation takes Jesus to
Jerusalem and to the pinnacle of the temple, where Satan asks him
to throw himself down. Once again Satan uses scripture to support
his temptations, citing Psalm 91:11-12: "For he shall give his angels
charge over thee, to keep thee in all thy ways. They shall bear thee
up in their hands, lest thou dash thy foot against a stone." If God is
who he says he is, and if Jesus is who he believes himself to be, and
if angels do what they are supposed to do, then why not engage in a
spectacular demonstration of all these truths? It would certainly attract attention and prove beyond all doubt that this was a God who
delivered the goods. Who can quarrel with asking God to be God
or at least to act like God? Some would argue that Karl Barth

created an entire theology out of the claim that we should "let God be God"; and if, as the song suggests, "His eye is on the sparrow, and I know he watches me," then what is wrong with putting that conviction to the test?

This provoking proposition appears like a pair of bookends in the public life of Jesus, for we encounter it again three years later when the so-called impenitent thief hanging on the cross alongside Jesus says to him, "If you are the son of God, come down from the cross, save yourself and us." In neither instance, though, is Jesus drawn into the maw of a false debate. In the first case, he replies with a biblical injunction against putting God to the test, and in the second, it is obedience to God's will rather than a desire to prove his or God's power that causes him to ignore the question and offer pardon to the thief, who confesses his sin and asks for forgiveness.

These are heroic encounters of a beleaguered but steadfast Jesus against a shrewd and persistent adversary, and the episode ends with Luke's chilling testimony to the perseverance of the devil: "And when the devil had ended every temptation, he departed from him until an opportune time."[5] We know it's not over, that there's a sequel to come, for the devil will not be fobbed off with quotations from the Bible. He waits for his moment and will strike again; the devil, as we must know by now, never gives up.

It is at the end of this ordeal, and flush with his power of overcoming it, that Jesus returns to his hometown. His reputation precedes him, and he teaches in the regional synagogues to great acclaim, obviously having emerged well from his season of testing. It can even be claimed that the testing and his survival of it made him an effective teacher and preacher, for, as is written elsewhere in the Gospels, he spoke with authority and not like just any teacher or rabbi. A reputation is a dangerous thing, however, for it raises expectations that may or may not have anything to do with the substance of the one whose reputation precedes him. What people think they know and what they want to believe fuel the creation of a person and a relationship that may have no basis in fact or reality; when that happens, sooner or later someone is bound to be disappointed, and with great disappointment often come serious consequences.

Rejection at Nazareth

We have seen, then, the setting for Jesus' sermon in his home synagogue, the sermon that started out so well and ended so badly; and perhaps it will be helpful to think of what follows in Luke 4 as a three-act play.

In Act 1, the charming and able young preacher is hailed by his family and friends. Who says you can't go home again? Of course you can, but you have to be prepared for changes beneath the patina of the familiar.

Act 2 involves the preaching of the sermon from scripture, the invocation of the prophet Isaiah, and the analysis and application of the text to the present circumstances. Here is where the trouble begins or, as is said in the black church, "The preacher ceases preachin' and starts meddlin'." When Jesus applies the truths of the text to the lives of those listening and, for example, immodestly states that "Today this scripture has been fulfilled in your hearing," the difficulties begin and the crisis of application takes place.

Act 3 is the reaction—swift, unhappy, and violent. People do not like to hear what they do not like to hear, and Jesus suffers more at the hands of his hometown congregation than he had at the hands of Satan a few verses earlier. His people would have killed him if they could have: to be dragged out of the pulpit and cast over a cliff by an angry congregation of your friends and neighbors is a pretty dramatic expression of disapproval. Had Jesus not earlier endured the greater threat to his soul, we might worry about this very real threat to his body, but in one of the greatest bits of understatement in all of scripture, Luke concludes the episode with these words at verse 30: "But passing through the midst of them he went away."

What was it, we may ask, that proved so offensive in Jesus' preaching as recorded in this account of his sermon in Nazareth? It may well have been the arrogance of youth. Jesus was, after all, a young man of thirty. Although he had acquired a reputation, he was still rather new among those who preached and taught, and it was this novelty that contributed to his reputation and the approbation of the crowds. He was young, which in a culture that cherished wisdom could be a liability, but in a crowd that is stimulated by novelty, youth can also be an asset. Youth, however, is not the issue; it is hard to think that Jesus' youth alone provoked the congregation's rage, even if one adds to it the natural hubris that goes with youth.

What set off his hometown congregation was the notion that the application of scripture, as Jesus made it in his sermon, disconfirmed rather than affirmed their sense of themselves. Having credited the preacher with a natural authority to speak to them, they were now obliged to listen to some unpleasant home truths, which in the minds of many, I suggest, trespassed upon their hospitality to their young itinerant preacher. We know that early in the discourse, at the exposition of the text and before the application, they heard him gladly, claiming him as one of their own. "Is not this Joseph's son?" they said. That itself is not a simple statement of genealogy, for in asking "Is not this Joseph's son?" they acknowledge what was surely known to them as the vexed paternity of Jesus. In a sense this is both an identification and a put-down, which becomes a compliment of the sort that says, "Considering who he is, he is doing very well indeed." There may even be a hint of cultural condescension here that prepares us for what follows in Act 3.

Perhaps I am too sensitive to this point, but I recall a remark made to me many years ago toward the close of two terms of my residency in a college of Cambridge University, England. It was at an end-of-term dinner, a splendid affair in the hall of Emmanuel College, of which college I have since become an Honorary Fellow. At the time I was, as I am now, a Harvard professor, and I had preached many times in the College Chapel and taken full part in the affairs of the Senior Common Room. After a slightly frosty reception at the beginning of my time in residence there, I had come to enjoy the banter of all and the friendship of many of the Fellows; perhaps needless to say, I was the only person of color on the premises. At this particular dinner, with the port having been freely consumed, the Domestic Bursar, a retired brigadier possessed of all the liabilities of a person of that ilk, said to me, "Well, Gomes, considering your background you've done very well here." Never have grace and malice been more subtly mixed and administered than they were then, and the comment put me in immodest remembrance of those lines from Luke 4, "Is not this Joseph's son?"

Thus, when it becomes clear who is speaking, the audacity of the application is all the more clear. What gave offense was the notion that, special as they were, God did not confine his mercies to them: the non-Jewish widow of Zarephath and Naaman the Syrian are held up as instances of God's generosity beyond the chosen few of the "chosen people."

A conventional reading of this passage suggests that the people were offended and driven to violent action because Jesus appeared to be making presumptuous claims about himself. This is Joseph's son, known to the villagers, and he is claiming messiahship. How dare he? The only appropriate response to blasphemy is to destroy the blasphemer. I think, however, that another view is in order: the people take offense not so much with what Jesus claims about himself, as with the claims he makes about a God who is more than their own tribal deity. Their good news must necessarily be bad news for somebody else; otherwise, what is the point of being a chosen and special people? Jesus offends the sensibilities of his hearers when he says that God is interested in people unlike themselves, such as the non-Jewish widow of Zarephath and Naaman, the Syrian aristocrat. It was not the issue of Jesus' claims about himself but rather his challenging the entitled identity of his hearers that drove them to fury. This is the sense of claim and offense that the hymn writer Samuel Johnson would capture centuries later when in 1864 he wrote what became a popular staple of Unitarian hymnody:

> *Life of ages, richly poured, love of God, unspent and free*
> *Flowing in the prophet's word, and the people's liberty.*
> *Never was to chosen race that unstinted tide confined;*
> *Thine is every time and place, fountain sweet of heart and mind.*

Jesus' sermon in Nazareth anticipates a famous little book by J. B. Phillips, *Your God Is Too Small.* What seemed to give the greatest offense was the notion that God was bigger than their conception of him, more generous than they were, and that this fact was at the heart of their own scriptures. This provoked what the therapeutic professions call an identity crisis. What is that? Well, if God isn't "ours," then who are we?

The Bigger God of the Gospel

Not long ago, when I found myself on a panel with Rick Warren, author of the fabulous book *The Purpose-Driven Life,* I told him that I was guilty of the sins of envy and covetousness: I envied his sales and coveted his royalties. He took the remark in good humor, as he could well afford to do. We were each asked a variety of questions, and our secular interrogators harped on the question of whether anyone can be saved who is not a born-again Christian. Rick's answer was as generous as his theology would allow, but the crux of the matter for him were the words in John's Gospel, "I am the way, the truth, and the life; no man cometh unto the Father but by me." He then threw the smoldering potato over to me, and I responded that I could not imagine that the God who is the creator of all has no plan of salvation for the billions of others in this world, and perhaps even beyond our galaxy, except for a New Testament one. Surely God has not forgotten those of his creation who are not Christians. Romans tells us that he certainly has not forgotten the Jews. "So," I said to my friend Rick, "I can only conclude that my God is bigger than yours."

That is something of the point that Jesus was trying to make in his sermon in Nazareth, and he would perhaps have reminded his fellow Jews that "our" God is bigger than we are. Although he did not finish that sermon, throughout the rest of his preaching and teaching, as recorded in Luke and in the other Gospels, the claim of a God bigger than those who worship him, more gracious, more generous, more hospitable than they are, is at the core of what Jesus calls the good news, or the gospel, and it *ought* to be good news that God is bigger than we are.

> *For we are weak, and need some deep revealing*
> *Of trust and strength and calmness from above.*[6]

The parables, Jesus' most effective teaching instruments, often place a generous God in counterdistinction to a less-than-generous human actor. The most famous parable of all, that of the Prodigal Son, is often restyled "The Waiting Father," since to the elder brother and perhaps to most listeners it is the father who is generosity incarnate, rushing to welcome home his estranged son and working to reconcile the elder brother to the new situation. In the parable of the workers in the vineyard, what is implicit is made explicit when these words are put into the mouth of the owner of the vineyard: "Am I not allowed to do what I choose with what belongs to me? Or are you envious because I am generous?"[7] This account ends with that most annoying and enigmatic of all biblical aphorisms, "The last will be first, and the first will be last."

Such a conclusion is bound to offend many who as a right regard themselves as first. We argue for equity and everyone is pleased to speak of a level playing field. In contemporary America, the argument against affirmative action is that it presumes, in the name of correction, to privilege some people over other people; and even in twenty-first-century, multicultured England it is still considered bad form to cut into a line or break into a queue. Thus, in the name of fair-mindedness and egalitarianism, the gospel's claim of a radical reordering, a redistribution, an exercise in almost Gilbertian topsy-turveydom, is an offense, a scandal, and hardly good news.

It is interesting to note that those who most frequently call for fair play are those who are advantaged by the play as it currently is, and that only when that position of privilege is endangered are they likely to benefit from the change required to "play by the rules." What if the "rules" are inherently unfair or simply wrong, or a greater good is to be accomplished by changing them? When the gospel says, "The last will be first, and the first will be last," despite the fact that it is counterintuitive to our cultural presuppositions, it is invariably good news to those who are last, and at least problematic news to those who see themselves as first.

This problem of perception is at the heart of a serious hearing of what Jesus has to say, and most people are smart enough to recognize that their immediate self-interest is served not so much by Jesus and his teaching as by the church and its preaching. Thus, it is no accident that although Jesus came preaching a disturbing and redistributive gospel, we do not preach what Jesus preached. Instead, we preach Jesus.

Desmond Tutu is fond of the African proverb that says that when the white Christians came to Africa they had the Bible and the Africans had the land. "Then," he says, "the Africans were given the Bible and the white Christians took the land." The legacy of worldwide colonialism is in many cases the pacification of a culture by the Bible, and the misappropriation of that culture by those who use the Bible as an instrument of control. For the Bible to be seen as an instrument of control rather than as one of liberation is to do violence to the substance of the Bible, but it is reassuring to those in whose interests the status quo stands. Why? Because the risk of displacement and transformation is too great. If the first shall be last and the last first, what happens to all of us who have spent every waking hour devising stratagems either to remain first or to become first? If our good news is always bad news for someone, we think, then let it be bad news for someone else and not for us.

When Jesus speaks of the good news in Luke 4:43—"I must preach the good news of the kingdom of God to the other cities also; for I was sent for this purpose"—he is not proclaiming the status quo as sacred but is promising that there is a new message and a new messenger. He comes not to confirm but to confront. The Bible may be put to the purposes of the comfortable, and perhaps never more so than in these early days of the twenty-first century, when the preaching of the comfortable by the comfortable, to and for the comfortable, floods every inspirational television and radio station in the world. The gospel, however, the radical words of Jesus properly understood in their full transformative power, is another story. If we understand the gospel aright, we too might be prepared to take violent action against Jesus and any who are bold enough to translate what he says into practice. It is to those implications of the good news as Jesus preached it that we now turn.

THREE

The Risks of Nonconformity

Our concern must be to live while we are alive ... to release our inner selves from the spiritual death that comes with living behind a façade designed to conform to eternal definitions of who and what we are.

—Elisabeth Kübler-Ross

Perhaps the most dangerous verse in all the Bible is the second verse of Romans 12, where Saint Paul endorses Christian nonconformity. When he writes, "And be not conformed to this world: but be ye transformed by the renewing of your mind, that ye may prove what is that good, and acceptable, and perfect, will of God," he is telling his readers not to do that which comes naturally to them. An invitation to nonconformity is a dangerous thing, and thoughtful nonconformity, for that is what Paul is requiring, is all the more dangerous because nonconformity is an intention and not an inadvertence. In a culture in which conformity is valued, nonconformity is likely to get one into trouble.

In the life of the English church in the aftermath of the Reformation, a nonconformist was one who refused to conform to the
norms of the Church of England, rejected the Act of Uniformity
and, for conscience' sake, read Romans 12 as an invitation to dissent from the political and theological compromises that united
church and state under the English crown. People who held this
view, the ancestors of those whom history would later call Puritans,
were known in their own time both as nonconformists and as dissenters. The pains and penalties attached to dissent and nonconformity were often severe; they included confiscation of property,
deprivation of civil liberties, banishment, and death. Nonconformity, in the eyes of those who see themselves as orthodox, encourages heresy, and heresy always means trouble for the heretic. Yet, is
it not the case that Romans 12 commends nonconformity, dissent,
and even heresy in the face of what the world values, and of which
it usually approves?

The tension between what Romans 12 says and what most people
believe is muted by the fact that most Christians read scripture
within the context of their own circles of faith and interpretation.
That is, despite all the claims of those who would wrap themselves
in biblical authority, most people read the Bible as confirmation of
their own practices and convictions; they do not find themselves
either condemned by it or challenged to change their views in light
of what it has to say. Thus, conformity or nonconformity does not
have to do with some abstract biblical principle or even the biblical
practices of some distant and distinct period. Rather, conformity has
to do with the current prevailing opinion and practice, and nonconformity departs from that cultural consensus. Godly conduct would
appear to be what the people of God say it is at any particular time,
just as in America the law is what the Supreme Court says it is.

This may seem a harsh indictment of those who would take the
Bible seriously, even literally, as so many American Christians claim

to do, yet how else does one explain the fact that the Bible and the church more often than not are used to preserve the status quo rather than to challenge or change it? The objections to Jesus' teaching, as we have already seen, were based on the view that he was an agent of change. "He stirreth up the people" was one of the charges shouted against him when Pilate asked why he should be condemned. The trouble with the apostles, who preached throughout the book of Acts, was that they were introducing new things into the moral discourse of the day. They themselves were ordinary, unlearned men, speaking out of place and out of turn, and for their pains they were persecuted, imprisoned, driven from place to place, and made to suffer all manner of terrible indignities. Hebrews 11 makes clear what the nonconformists suffered:

> They were stoned, they were sawn asunder, were tempted, were slain with the sword: they wandered about in sheepskins and goatskins, being destitute, afflicted, tormented ...[1]

That the image of martyrs, the suffering faithful, and oppressed witnesses to the truth does not seem to be the prevailing image of Christians in the world either in ancient or modern times serves to demonstrate the sad fact that conformity is a greater characteristic of the Christian community than nonconformity.

The people described in the Bible as people of faith are usually depicted as those whose loyalty to their faith places them on the outside of the prevailing culture, and their rules and practices are designed both to distinguish them and to protect them against that culture. Biblical people are by definition people on the margins who are, in the classical aphorism, *contra mundum*, against the world. If the world is Egypt or Rome, then religious people, Jews or Christians, are against that, distinct from it, and defining themselves in opposition to it. Conformity to that world and its values is death. When it is said, in the First Epistle General of John, "Love not the world, neither the things that are in the world," the meaning is that one is not to be taken in by the natural charms and desires of the world to which it is so easy to conform.

When Paul speaks of nonconformity in Romans, he is speaking of a world easily defined as distinct from what we might call today the Christian worldview. Paul, however, was not inviting social revolution, a point that such Christian conservatives as Martin Luther were always eager to make. His principle was one of nonconformity, but his call to obedience to the magistrate was one of expedience. That situation is similar to the position in which Christian slaves found themselves in the American antebellum south when, in order to survive, the slaves had to give outward obedience to their masters. They knew, however, that to conform to the slave culture was itself a form of death, and so their real survival depended upon their ability to be loyal to something else and other. Their virtue as believers was defined by their distinction from those who held power over them.

What happens when the minority and the oppressed become the majority with the capacity to oppress others? Where, then, is the mandate for nonconformity? How then does one read Romans 12? Where, in a minority status, nonconformity can be seen as courageous and heroic, when the minority becomes a majority, nonconformity becomes dangerous, seditious, heretical.

The Trouble with Power

At a gathering of clergy I advanced the not particularly welcome view that the Christian church as contemplated in the gospels was never intended to prevail in this world. The church's transformation from a virtuous minority to an oppressive majority was not an anticipation of earthly success. The earthly status of the church was described as the "church militant," still waging a struggle against the world, whereas the "church triumphant" referred to the church in heaven. This distinction, although lost on many who longed for the earthly triumph of the church, nevertheless remains a point worth remembering. To some, the temporal triumph of the Christian community in the world is a sign of God's favor and the essential righteousness of the Christian position. The irony of the matter, though, is that whenever the Christian community gains worldly power, it nearly always loses its capacity to be the critic of the power and influence it so readily brokers. When the pre-Reformation reformers looked at the worldly power and success of the Roman Catholic church in the West—and even considering the glories of Western civilization that the church did so much to advance—the comparison with its New Testament and primitive antecedents was so striking that true reformation meant a return to the days of relative poverty and powerlessness, to a community more recognizable to Jesus, the apostles, and the patriarchs than the contemporary papal empire with all its worldly success.

Thus the tension, consistently inherent in the religious community, is between what it takes to be successful in the world and what it means to be faithful to a world that is not yet, and therefore nonconforming to the world that is. Sometimes that tension is resolved by the notion of otherworldliness that obtains here and now. The old gospel song puts it in words familiar to many:

This world is not my home,
I'm just passing through;
My treasures are laid up
Somewhere beyond the blue:
The angels beckon me
From Heaven's open door;
And I can't feel at home
In this world any more.

Often, Christians have been criticized for this strain of other-worldliness. Being ill at ease in this world and longing for another suggests an inattention, even an indifference, to the problems of this world, and the sins of irresponsibility and poor stewardship are invoked. We are reminded that in the prayer Jesus taught, he urged that God's will be done "on earth, as it is in heaven."

That criticism has stuck with many, and the whole tradition of attempting to make heaven on earth comes as an attempt to address it. Instead of longing for the time that is to be, a strong and endur-ing Christian tradition argues that we should make earth, this world, in Saint Augustine's felicitous phrase, a "colony of heaven." Thus, the idea of ideal religious communities, where Christian vir-tues are practiced in contradistinction to the world, became an im-portant part of the religious life. The very term "religious life," as applied to the communities of monks and nuns, referred to a way so nonconforming to the ways of the world that separate rules, dress, and expectations were mandated to distinguish those within that life from those outside in the world. It is true that life within those formal religious communities was predicated on a high degree of confor-mity: one did not "do one's own thing" within the community, which would be dangerous and destructive. The very community—monastery, nunnery, abbey—was distinguished by its nonconfor-mity to the larger world from which it had withdrawn.

Puritanism in the New World was an attempt to construct an ideal community within which faith could be practiced in contrast to the religious conformity required by the Church of England. The nonconformist colonies of Plymouth, Massachusetts, in 1620 and Massachusetts Bay in 1630 were not designed to be havens of tolerance, but were meant to be models of how a particular people could live as an ideal community both in the world and against it. What made their efforts interesting had little to do with their own intolerance of those who failed to conform to their vision of community; they were not professing tolerance, and so they cannot be charged with hypocrisy in failing to practice it. What made them interesting was their understanding that their witness depended upon how they appeared to those to whom they refused to conform. Governor Bradford of Plymouth saw his fledgling colony's attempt at the holy experiment of godly living as "one small candle," in his now famous phrase, and hoped that its light would shine in such a way that the world would see how this enterprise in nonconformity worked. A decade later, Governor Winthrop, in what is perhaps the most famous sermon ever given in English, declared that the Puritan experiment over which he presided should be seen as a "city on a hill," a reference to Jesus' Sermon on the Mount. He fully expected that

> ... the eyes of all people are upon us; so that if we shall deal falsely with our God in this work we have undertaken, and so cause Him to withdraw His present help from us, we shall be made a story and a by-word through the world.

His sermon, "A New Modell of Christian Charity," was preached aboard the *Arbella*, the lead ship of the landing fleet, and in it Winthrop upheld as a model a community that would be defined by its nonconformity to the ways of the Old World. The Old World would be compelled to conform. Through such cultural nonconformity, the Old World would be transformed.

For nonconformity to work in the transforming fashion suggested by Saint Paul in Romans 12, there must be something against which both the Christian and the Christian community can be compared, and by which their own distinctive traits can be seen in significant contrast. What happens, however, when the Christian community and the culture to which it must not conform become intermixed? Even more risky, what happens when the Christian culture becomes at one with the secular culture, when the interests of one become the same as the interests of the other, and nonconformity becomes a danger, a threat, and a risk?

Reform and Dissent

In nineteenth-century America, movements for social reform often came out of the ambition to make the world more like the church, corresponding insofar as possible with the mandate of the Lord's Prayer. With the power to persuade, and eventually to compel, Christians sought to reform society through such movements as temperance, women's rights, public education, and the abolition of slavery. Each of those efforts encountered strong resistance, much of it based on biblical grounds. The debates, however, were not between a nonconformist minority religious community and an all-powerful state, but largely within what had by that time become "Christian society," wherein the conventional wisdom of Christianity, although variously interpreted, prevailed. Nonconformists shared in the rule of the culture. The American Civil War was fought by Christian communities with differing views on the moral and biblical case for or against slavery. To many today, the obvious Christian position was abolitionist, but that was not the case in the days leading up to Fort Sumter. Nothing angered southerners more than to be regarded as less than Christian because of their commitment to chattel slavery.

Earlier in the nineteenth century, when the New England churches, heirs of seventeenth-century Puritanism, split along Trinitarian and Unitarian lines, both parties to the dispute were firmly identified with the establishment of the day, and although the Trinitarians frequently referred to the Unitarians as heretics, they were hardly so in the sense of dissenting from the cultural establishment. Despite the fact that local mapmakers often referred to the Trinitarians as the "orthodox" church, implying that the Unitarians were the nonconformists, the true dissenters or nonconformists were neither Unitarian nor Trinitarian Congregational; they were the Quakers, the Baptists, and even the Episcopalians, who had not inherited their places in the cultural establishment.

Dissent from the status quo became a way of life, and as the Christian community became increasingly identified with the larger culture, it became even more important to establish a unique identity in dissent from it. Ralph Waldo Emerson is often regarded as an example of theological nonconformity, and in a memorable address to the Harvard Divinity School he urged a stout resistance to the orthodoxy of the day when he invited his hearers to "acquaint thyself at first hand with Deity." Theodore Parker, who as a student had heard the address, would himself become a nonconformist even to Emerson's nonconformity. Of Parker it would be said of his relationship to the Unitarian Christians of his day, "From their orthodox dissent, he dissented."

Rather than a point of pride, the tradition of Christian dissent and nonconformity seems to be an embarrassment. The flourishing of orthodoxies and the Christian community's enchantment with power form a dangerous combination of forces that make Paul's appeal to nonconformity difficult for the Christian to take seriously. It is even more difficult for the non-Christian to believe that the Christian could possibly take it seriously.

Some years ago I attended a White House Prayer Breakfast. I didn't particularly want to go, but a former student of mine, well placed in the Clinton White House, prevailed upon me to attend, and so I did—and immediately knew I had made the wrong decision when I found myself in a long line of clergy in the street opposite the Treasury, waiting to have our credentials validated for admission into the White House. What a sight we must have been to early morning Washington commuters! Every conceivable form of clerical dress from nearly all the religions of the world was represented, and all the people so dressed were eager for a moment of favor in the East Room of the White House. Once we were inside, it was worse—a sort of early morning clerical cocktail party comprised of clergy hoping to be seen with anyone more important than the person with whom they happened to be speaking. There was little prayer at this Prayer Breakfast, but a great deal of networking and schmoozing, and whatever Caesar had to offer, the clergy were glad to take it. A convention of almost any other group would have had more grace than this assemblage of the clergy, with its unsubtle ambition to see and be seen. No one in the assemblage seemed to embrace a nonconformist thought: the world appeared very much in charge. Both John the Baptist and David Koresh would have been out of place, and I, no prophetic soul, wished I were anywhere but there.

Prayer Breakfasts are a big deal in Washington, I am told, and foreign visitors who are brought to them are fascinated by both their absence of piety and their display of power. Most of those who bow their heads before tucking into the eggs and bacon are not seeking transformation, but rather appear to be celebrating the confirmation of the status quo or, worse, longing to recreate the good old days when a Christian consensus determined the right and wrong ways of doing things.

Christian conservatism suggests that there were good old days, and much of the momentum behind a good deal of contemporary religious zealotry is an attempt to recapture something of what was lost. The notion of revival, a recurrent theme in American religious history, appeals to that notion of something that once was good that must somehow be recovered.

Revival or Renewal

To someone who takes the good news seriously, the notion of revival is a problem, a conceit to suggest that at one time we had "it," we have now lost "it," and we are seeking to get "it" again. As a historian, I am often asked to what great period in history I would care to return, and I can think of none, for every age has fallen short of what the good news promised, and no past age has achieved an instance of grace for which I would sacrifice one second of the future. When I say, as I often do, that our best days are ahead of us, I truly believe that the good news that Jesus preached has yet to be experienced, for it goes before us, as did Jesus himself on Easter morning.

Now, I understand the power of nostalgia, especially where religion is concerned. For more than forty years I have presided over an annual summer hymn sing in which the congregation has an opportunity to belt out the old hymns of the faith from years gone by. People who profess to believe in little or nothing will nonetheless spend an hour singing until they are hoarse the songs their grandparents knew and loved, hymns such as "I Love to Tell the Story," "When Peace Like a River," "Blessed Assurance, Jesus Is Mine," "When the Roll Is Called Up Yonder, I'll Be There," and on and on. No one knows those songs better than I, or loves them more, and there is something akin to magic in the air when in a small country church at the close of the day nearly one hundred souls spanning all the generations sing those songs to the heavens. Surely "There Is Power in the Blood," and in this emotion, but the point to remember is that we experience our joy, or at least most of us do, in catching something of a time gone by, whereas our ancestors sang the songs in anticipation of something yet to come. We tend to consecrate the past, but they hallowed the future, or, as I am fond of saying to friends who delight in the historical: our yesterday was their tomorrow.

"Revival" is not the word, for that credits the past with too much. The word that suggests that it is not yet over is not "revival," but "renewal." I happen to be a great admirer of The Reverend Billy Graham. Twice I have invited him to preach at Harvard University, and twice he has accepted; and by my invitations I have managed to offend my secular friends who consider Billy Graham "too religious" for Harvard, my pluralist friends who consider him "too Christian" for Harvard, and my liberal friends who consider him "too conservative" for Harvard. My conservative friends were suspicious on general principles. Billy Graham's visits, however, were triumphs. The first time he came, he gave as his sermon title "Peace in a Nuclear Age," since he had just returned from the old Soviet Union at a time when disarmament was the great desire for civilization. The Memorial Church was filled to the doors and a live relay was arranged for the overflow, for it seemed that everybody wanted to hear what Billy Graham had to say at Harvard about peace in the nuclear age. When they realized that he was still asking them to receive Jesus as the key to both inner peace and world peace, they went away "sorrowful and disappointed," like the rich young ruler of the biblical story.

The second time he came to Harvard, almost a decade later, Billy Graham was visibly afflicted with Parkinson's disease and began his sermon with perhaps the most arresting opening statement any preacher has ever made: "I know I am going to die, but I'm not worried. Are you?" Well, that got our attention, and we listened intently to a sermon that was a call to renewal. Billy Graham is said to have reinvented the revival in our time, beginning with his first crusade in New York City nearly sixty years ago; he has said that he has only one sermon, and he preaches it over and over again. There is something we all want, need, and have never had, so he is not calling us to an old but to a new life. The invitation that he has made famous by associating it with the hymn "Just as I Am," and the image of thousands streaming from the stands to make a commitment to Christ, suggests that what we seek is before us, not behind us. Renewal means trying again to lay hold upon the promise that tomorrow is better than yesterday; and that is indeed good news.

Some years ago, a study was done of those who accepted Billy Graham's altar calls at the large urban rallies held by him around the world, and among the things the study revealed was that any number of people who came forward at the meetings had done so before. It was not that they were like "professional mourners," people who as a matter of routine went forward, nor was it an admission that their first response hadn't "taken." Some of those interviewed noted that they went forward again and again because they found themselves renewed, empowered, and encouraged each time. In other words, they understood that religious commitment is a process and not a one-time event, that each time they heard and responded to the call they were in a different place than they had been previously. They were engaged in a movement, and each call brought them nearer the goal.

Critics of revivals, such as those in which the same people often come forward, have argued that it is obvious that such meetings don't work. Billy Graham and others reply, however, with this telling analogy: "Just because one bath works is no reason not to take another."

At the heart of the best evangelical preaching is an invitation to the future, and an opportunity to try that which has never been tried before. At its best, evangelical Christianity invites us into terra incognita, an unknown land where we move not by sight but by faith.

Alas, in much that passes for evangelical preaching these days, that impulse for the new and untried is lost in a rhetoric of personal security, political power, and cultural nostalgia. That is too bad, for the great success of the evangelical movement in modern American religious life suggests that millions are hungering and thirsting for genuine good news that will take them beyond the alleged securities of the status quo and into a promised land not yet experienced. The great question is, Can these megachurches, television preachers, and Bible empires deliver the goods? From what orthodoxies do these movements dissent? What transformations do they offer? What conformities do they shatter, and to what larger, even subversive, loyalty do they appeal?

John W. Dean's fifteen minutes of fame came under exacting circumstances and at a terrible price. When he is remembered today, it is because in an earlier life he was the White House counsel to President Richard M. Nixon and played a pivotal role in the constitutional crisis known as Watergate. Unlike many of the key players in that sorry episode, Dean has not turned his attention to religion but has been concerned with the witches' brew of conservative Republican politics and conservative religion, an admixture of interests and convictions for which his old superior bears more than a passing responsibility. In his book, *Conservatives Without Conscience*, Dean speaks to the transformation of the conservative in American life and calls that transformation "the triumph of the authoritarians." In an op-ed piece in *The Boston Globe*, Dean cites one of his sources as saying that authoritarian conservatives are "... enemies of freedom, anti-democratic, anti-equality, highly prejudiced, mean-spirited, power hungry, Machiavellian, and amoral."[2]

This description does not apply strictly to those religious persons who call themselves conservatives. To those, however, who have observed the so-called religious right's rise in political influence over the past quarter of a century, the similarities are both familiar and frightening. Political conservatives derive their power from the mobilization of constituencies that feel deprived of their rightful share in government, and regard the cultural consensus against which they fight to be the wrong one.

I remember listening to a young and impassioned Ralph Reed, who rightly is credited with mobilizing the forces of this discontent into a political movement, a feat that neither The Reverend Jerry Falwell nor The Reverend Pat Robertson alone could accomplish. Speaking of what he called the "coarsening" of America, Ralph Reed argued that something had to be done to reclaim a civil, decent America. The face of that revived America would look very Republican and very Protestant, or, at least, Christian. In Reed's view, the countervailing pleas for diversity suggested a weakness of will, and calls for tolerance suggested an indifference to truth and to what was right. Thus, in the name of restoring civil civic discourse, strong measures would have to be taken: religion of the right sort would become more militant, more ambitious for a worldly agenda, more willing to stake its claims to a place in the public square—and eventually to the public square itself.

The political and cultural consequences of this move to what some have called the religious right have given rise to the claims of many that we are in one of our periodic American "great awakenings." By this, religious pundits mean that we are once again in a period in which the revival of religion is a national phenomenon. The so-called values voters of 2004 were to many a sure sign of this, and the growth of large nondenominational churches, the so-called megachurches, together with evangelicals, is a force with which to be reckoned in the culture.

It is true that there is a great deal of religion about these days, but to call it a revival is hardly accurate, for this phenomenon is not the summoning from slumber of something that once was, but the introduction of a religious sensibility quite different from what we have experienced in the past. It is not simply "old-time religion" that is getting a new lease and influence on life. As any sociologist of religion will be quick to tell, there are more varieties of religious experience alive and flourishing in America today than Jonathan Edwards, Charles G. Finney, or even Billy Graham could have guessed at the height of their revivalist activities. This is not the Protestantism of our grandparents, nor is it the theocratic dream of many who see America as God's chosen place on earth. Add to this the whole enterprise of those for whom religion itself is now superseded by something called "spirituality," and we find ourselves in a remarkably different religious place than our ancestors ever imagined.

Modesty and Charity

When we consider this new religious sensibility, what are the implications for Christians and others who are concerned for the welfare of a culture that is increasingly seduced by the values of materialism, entertainment, and the general coarsening of discourse but are not prepared to retreat into a kind of religious absolutism rooted in a cultural nostalgia or a tinny patriotism?

Increasingly, I meet people who, when asked, "Are you a Christian?" respond with the parsing carefulness of a lawyer, or of Bill Clinton: "That depends on what you mean by Christian." Many say, "I would like to think of myself as a Christian, but I don't want to be associated with [this group or that group]." Many complain that the evangelicals have defined "Christian" in such a way as to impose a creed and not a lifestyle. In the early church a Christian was one who believed, on the authority of the witnesses to the resurrection, that Jesus is Lord. In the early twentieth century, some Christians, eventually described as fundamentalists, imposed a series of fundamental beliefs essential to being a Christian, including a belief in the literal truth of scripture, the virgin birth, the second coming, and substitutionary atonement. Those who affirmed those things were Christians; those who did not, were not. In the summer of 2006, at the Aspen Institute, I heard Ted Haggard, at that time senior pastor of an evangelical megachurch in Colorado and president of the National Association of Evangelicals, define a Christian as one who believes in the literal truth of scripture, in Jesus as personal Lord and Savior, and in being born again.

In the 1920s, Harry Emerson Fosdick condemned fundamentalism for its lack of charity and its refusal to share disputed ground with Christians of other persuasions. Can Christians agree that following the teachings of Jesus and the example that he and the best of his followers have set is sufficient to maintain a Christian identity and witness in the world? It would seem not. It can be argued that in the first decade of the twenty-first century, Christians have either lost their nerve—that is, they deny any unique or normative contribution to the world—or they expect the world to conform to a Christian worldview. In other words, there is no serious belief system outside their own: it's either "my way"—which is God's way—"or the highway."

Fosdick predicted that the kind of narrow, doctrinal piety with which he associated the aggressive fundamentalism of his day would expire in the light of modernity and higher education. He would be surprised, and perhaps more than a little disappointed, to find that the modernist position that he espoused has long been in retreat, and that the cultural tune is more often called by an evangelical piety having much in common with the fundamentalism to which he was so adamantly opposed. The mainline, as the old bromide has it, has become the sideline, and the question remains, Now that Christianity is increasingly defined in terms agreeable to evangelicals, what does this kind of Christianity look like?

It looks like power, influence, and a new establishment. The old fringe is now the new center, and one of the great risks to a new establishment is the danger inherent in dissent and nonconformity.

This returns us to our familiar theme that in religion, as in much else, good news for some is almost always bad news for others. Two elements nearly always missing from any religious establishment, especially one that has come to prevail only after a long period of suffering and deprivation in the wilderness, are charity and modesty. Charity is the capacity to love the other and to lead with the heart and not simply with the head. Although religious establishments often espouse charity, they rarely risk their own hard-won status by exercising it among others. Charity in this context often suggests weakness, a tolerance of error, a failure to exercise the sovereignty of truth. Charity free of condescension is rare. The best that one can hope for is the old aphorism: "You worship God in any way you choose, and I will worship him in his way." Religious establishments are terrified by any hint of relativism, and the notion that God may know more about the salvation business than we do is often more than a true believer can bear. Having won the truth "our" way, it is difficult to believe that there is any other way, or that anyone else might have found it.

Christian exclusiveness, for that is what the lack of charity suggests, cannot face the requirements of modesty, the notion that all is not known and that we do not know all. When devout Christians believe that only Christians of a particular doctrinal stripe have access to God, that, for example, God hears their prayers only, they stand in cosmic immodesty. The Christian Bible more than once makes the point that God's ways are not our ways, and that the mind of God is vastly different from our own minds. Thus, when Christians state categorically that Jews, or Muslims, or believers in other faith systems are outside the provisions of God, they utter arrogant nonsense. A respectful agnosticism is called for when often there is offered in its place a self-interested certainty. If God is the God of all, and not just a tribal deity, then God has made provision, not necessarily known to us, for the healing and care of all his creation, and not simply our little part of it.

J. B. Phillips observed many years ago that one's God is too small if within God's providence there is no care and awareness of the other. This is what the hymn writer F. W. Faber meant in "There's a Wideness in God's Mercy," when he said:

> *For the love of God is broader*
> *Than the measure of our mind;*
> *And the heart of the Eternal*
> *Is most wonderfully kind.*

If there is any good news that is truly good news for everybody, and not just for a few somebodies, it is this: God is greater and more generous than the best of those who profess to know and serve him. This is the radical nonconformity with the conventional wisdom that Jesus both proclaimed and exemplified, and, alas, it cost him his life. Will we hope to fare any better, as disciples of his nonconformity?

FOUR

What Would Jesus Have Me Do?

No doubt a life of Jesus should be written on one's knees, with a feeling of unworthiness great enough to make the pen drop from the hand. A sinner should blush for his temerity in undertaking such a work.

—François Mauriac,
Life of Jesus

In the last few years of the twentieth century, it became fashionable among certain religious people to wear jewelry inscribed with the letters *WWJD?* This was short for "What Would Jesus Do?" and it suggested a certain kind of personal ethic that predicated one's behavior on seeking guidance from Jesus in the decisions of daily life. The question, which was subjected to a certain amount of ridicule and parody, gave rise to additional questions such as "Would Jesus drive a Lexus, a Humvee, or a fuel-efficient model car?" "Would Jesus bomb suspected terrorist outposts, or would he favor negotiations?" and "Would Jesus vote for Republicans or Democrats?" Presumably, the answer was to be determined from a study of Jesus' words and actions as found in scripture, but more often than not the answer was determined by the presuppositions or predilections of the person asking the question. Both religious liberals and religious conservatives assumed that Jesus would behave as they did, that he would share their own prejudices and practices.

I, for one, have always thought this questionable slogan to be ill-put, for we are not Jesus and thus are unlikely to be able to know what he would do, or to do what he did. The human nature of Jesus notwithstanding, few of us would be able to act as he did even in similar circumstances; the appeal to Jesus as a human example has seemed to me to be an impossible goal. It is always difficult for us to follow the example of most of our human heroes, such as George Washington, Abraham Lincoln, Nelson Mandela, and Mother Teresa, for who could live up to their expectations? As a child, I rejoiced in reading the orange-backed series of potted biographies of American heroes, and, like Benjamin Franklin, I even tried to keep a journal. I tried never to tell a lie, like the young George Washington, known to be a truth-teller from Parson Weems's account of George and the famous cherry tree. I wanted to be as morally responsible as Abraham Lincoln, who walked miles to return a borrowed book; and I hoped to be as brave as Teddy Roosevelt when he charged up San Juan Hill. Soon, however, I put all of this down to a growing sense of maturity, and realized that those exemplary persons were just that—sources of inspiration but not models of possible conduct.

In college, in the days when reading the works of "dead white males" was still mandatory and not suspect, I encountered Plato's objection to young people reading about the Greek gods and goddesses on the grounds that those mythic figures were not exemplary enough, and furthermore displayed all-too-human character flaws and dysfunctional personalities. To me the gods were interesting precisely because of their human—and thus imperfect—qualities.

When I read about Jesus in the Gospels, the parts that always made sense to me were those situations in which he performed less than ideally or perfectly. When I was a child I found Jesus to be most real when he abandoned his parents for a much more interesting question-and-answer session with the doctors in the temple. As we all remember, his parents were first made anxious by his absence, and then angry when they discovered that he preferred the company of others to theirs. Although he was only twelve years old, he showed no contrition for causing his parents distress, and while he offered them an explanation, he gave no apology. Then there was the temper tantrum he had in the temple when he overturned the money-changers' table and expelled those who were doing lawful business selling doves and making change. Jesus was clearly angry, and all the preaching I had heard about his spiritual authority did not explain this frustration and anger. The violence of his actions was certainly out of character with the usual image of Jesus as a gentle persuader. I must confess that this little bit of ecclesiastical deviancy appealed to me as a child, and not because it was exemplary behavior, which it was not, but because it was such fundamentally human behavior.

How many Good Friday sermons have tried to address the words of doubt, anger, and even fear that Jesus cries out on the cross in the words of Psalm 22, "My God, my God, why hast thou forsaken me?" Certainly he was quoting scripture, but the scripture he quotes begins, as do many of the psalms, with a querulous and all-too-human doubt in God's reliability and presence. Any of Hollywood's leading men would make a far more heroic Jesus than Jesus himself, for the Jesus who fears in the garden and doubts on the cross is an embarrassment to many who yearn for a more heroic figure. Dietrich Bonhoeffer would make a better Christ figure than Jesus, for the purpose of a heroic victim.

When people ask "What Would Jesus Do?" they do not usually have those nonheroic moments in mind, nor does it seem that they would be particularly prepared to follow the example of Jesus in other matters. It is not an easy thing to forgive one's enemies, for example, yet Jesus does exactly that from the cross when he asks forgiveness for those who are busily crucifying him: "Father, forgive them, for they know not what they do." What Jesus does does not square with what we would do, or even with what we would want him to do.

In the student troubles of 1969 at Harvard, my late and good friend Archie Epps, then dean of students, was forcibly and with some violence ejected from his office in University Hall by a cadre of zealous students who seized the building as a trophy in their war against the establishment. On the thirtieth reunion of the class of 1969, a small group of now middle-aged alumni approached the dean and asked if, after all these years, bygones could be bygones. The dean, known for his irenic temperament and soft-spoken demeanor, replied, "As a Christian, I forgive you, but as a dean, I shall never forget." That may not have been an entirely Christ-like response, but I remember how much sense it made to me.

When Jesus speaks about the care of the poor, when he associates with those of low social caste, when he tells people not to worry about clothing, food, and drink, when he enunciates his ethic in the Sermon on the Mount, when he advises that we turn the other cheek, and when he says that the chief ethical activity is love, most of us of a certain age find that what he says squares with our own natural response to similar situations. In an analysis of why traditional stories about Jesus do not appeal to contemporary young people, however, I read that one respondent said that, according to what he read in the Bible, Jesus was a wimp. Jesus would never make it in the average American high school, the respondent suggested, and therefore trying to do what Jesus did is either impossible, as he is, after all, the son of God, or undesirable, for in terms of the world he doesn't win.

A New Formulation

The dilemma about what Jesus would do is avoided, or at least compromised, if the question is put differently and, in my view, as Jesus himself put it in the Gospels. The question should not be "What would Jesus do?" but rather, and more dangerously, "What would Jesus have me do?" The onus is not on Jesus but on us, for Jesus did not come to ask semidivine human beings to do impossible things. He came to ask human beings to live up to their full humanity; he wants us to live in the full implications of our human gifts, and that is far more demanding. Anyone can evade responsibility by attempting the impossible and failing; what Jesus asks is that we do what is possible, and that is the challenge that makes life interesting. Jesus does not ask us to behave as he did; he asks us to behave as we ought—which is why asking "What would Jesus have me do?" is far riskier than asking what Jesus himself would do. It might very well be as Thomas Merton writes: "It seems to me that I have greater peace and am closer to God when I am not 'trying to be a contemplative,' or trying to be anything special, but simply orienting my life fully and completely towards what seems to be required of a man like me at a time like this."

In a little book called *What Jesus Meant*, Garry Wills argues that Jesus is far more radical and dangerous than those who would domesticate him for their own purposes dare to believe. Both Christian socialists and biblical theocrats have something to fear—and something to learn—from the radical Jesus of the Gospels. Thomas

Jefferson, Wills reminds us, found the divine Jesus of the miracle and the supernatural simply too much for the rational mind of the eighteenth century. In his version of the New Testament, Jefferson got rid of all those unpalatable phenomena and turned Jesus into a teacher of ethics and morality, the Jesus of the Beatitudes and not of the Passion. There are many for whom this is an agreeable portrayal: Jesus as the great teacher of righteousness joins all the other great moral pedagogues, and from his wisdom and example we mine what is useful for our own lives, determining which truths are confined to their time period and which are timeless.

Karl Marx, it is said, objected to Christianity not because it was untrue but because it did not live out its own truth. Christian socialism was an effort to apply the teachings of Jesus to the operations of society without the interventions of the church or of Christian theology, and it was in this sense that the Roman Catholic church regarded communism as a heresy, a partial and incomplete version of Christian truth. Communism was guilty of a number of heresies and errors, not the least of which were its idolatry of the state, its denial of individual human dignity, and its totalitarianism, but what made communism—and socialism, its less pathological relation—appealing was the similarity rather than the dissimilarity that it bore to the Christian gospel and the fundamental teachings of Jesus.

Once, in a sermon, I cited without attribution the Marxian aphorism "From each according to his ability, to each according to his need" and asked if anyone knew who had said it. Most people thought that it came from somewhere in the Bible, and many ascribed it to Jesus. Why was this so? As one person said to me, "It sounds like something he would say." When I revealed that it was Karl Marx who had said it, those who believed me were profoundly disturbed. How could Jesus be confused with Karl Marx? Surely this was the work of the devil who, in classical theology, is referred to as the Old Deluder because of his capacity to confuse the faithful. Jesus and Marx could not have that much in common.

At Harvard the tradition of a daily service of Morning Prayers continues to flourish, and often a student offers the five-minute address that forms the heart of this fifteen-minute service at the beginning of the day. One day, one of our most attractive undergraduates gave the address, offering his testimony, describing how he had come to believe that it is better to give than to receive, that love is stronger than death, that good ultimately overcomes evil, that the love of money is bad, and that peace is the ultimate destiny for the created order. We listened to him in reverent devotion, and then came his ultimate line, when he said that because of all this he was therefore, in this most Christian of all places, a communist. Jaws dropped, eyes rolled, some of our most devout people were horrified, and I was asked to never allow him to speak again. "Why not?" I asked; "did he not speak a truth to which we all could subscribe?" He did, and we could, but to ascribe that truth to communism rather than to the Christian faith was just too much for those who saw the two positions as antagonistic and antiethical. At the risk of confirming already hardened opinions about "The People's Republic of Cambridge," I can say that I have never heard a better expression of the Christian faith. My only concern is that it didn't come from a Christian.

Actually, I live daily with a painful reminder of the price one pays for loyalty to the counterculture. On the south wall of Harvard's Memorial Church is an enormous tablet dedicated to alumni who died in World War II. It is an impressive roster of names, starting with Franklin Delano Roosevelt, of the class of 1904, who died as commander in chief and is rightly styled a war casualty. One name on the wall, however, stands out, and that is the name of a Divinity

School graduate, Adolf Sannwald, who has an asterisk beside his name with the notation "Enemy Casualty." His is a fascinating and sad story.

Adolf Sannwald was a German national who graduated from Harvard Divinity School and was killed while in the German army on the eastern front, in the campaign against Russia. Many look at his name and see a generous university that remembers its son who died under opposite colors, and it was with that quiet pride that I regarded the name of this lone German for many years, until one day I received a letter from a relative of his on the occasion of the fiftieth anniversary of the end of World War II. The writer noted that she had been proud that her relative's name appeared on the wall of honor at Harvard until she was informed that he was described as an enemy casualty. She then told me his story. Sannwald returned to Germany in the late 1930s after his time at Harvard and became a minister of the German Lutheran church, the confessing church in which such men as Dietrich Bonhoeffer were also clergy. Sannwald preached against national socialism, or the Nazi party, and became such a thorn in the flesh of the Nazi establishment that he was arrested. Rather than being sent to prison he was drafted into the German army and sent into the front lines of the brutal campaign in Russia, which was tantamount to a death sentence, and early in the campaign he died. The letter noted that he died for principles that stood in stark opposition to those of the powers-that-be, and that thus the final insult was to be described forever in the West, at his alma mater, as an enemy casualty.

What to do? I took the matter up with the Harvard authorities, but the fact remained that Sannwald was a member of the German army who died in combat. "How many asterisks can we put up?" the then-secretary of the university asked me in bureaucratic frustration, and so the name stands today, a monument to the price that conscience pays when it does not square with what the world requires.

Establishing New Priorities

Our situation would be easier if Jesus were less clear about the priorities he sets for us. As Mark Twain is said to have remarked, "It is not what I don't understand in the Bible that troubles me; it is what is perfectly clear that does." At the heart of the Sermon on the Mount in Matthew's Gospel, Jesus says, "But seek ye first the kingdom of God, and his righteousness; and all these things shall be added unto you."[1] "All these things" refers to such things as food, clothing, and other fundamental necessities of life, plus security, safety, and moral clarity. The priority that Jesus asks us to seek is God's kingdom, God's righteousness, the first thing above all else to which we are meant to direct our attention and efforts. That is also the first petition in the pattern of prayer that Jesus taught his followers to say: "Thy kingdom come, thy will be done ..." We should notice that only after that priority is established are we encouraged to ask for our own needs, in the form of daily bread; only after we have established the priority of the kingdom are we to attend to matters of economics: "Forgive us our debts, as we forgive our debtors ..."; and only after the priority of the kingdom are we encouraged to worry about temptation and evil. Even the future age, the coming "power and glory," happens within the context of what we can call "kingdom priority."

If the kingdom of God and his righteousness are given priority, all other things will fall into place and be seen in their proper perspective. This is called, for lack of a better term, the long view, for only in taking a long view can we avoid the tyranny of the moment and the terror of the immediate. Through the long view we can obtain a perspective that gives a better sense of proportion to the time being.

In the sense of the gospel, the good news is that in the long term, by the long view, God reigns, and that means that despite the troubles of the moment and the difficulties of the time, God's justice will prevail. This long view of the divine perspective allows the human being confidence when there would appear to be no immediate reason for confidence. The powerful witness of the early Christian martyrs was that in the face of torment, torture, and every reason for fear, they faced death not overwhelmed by the moment but confident that in the long view God would prevail, their deaths would have meaning, and so would their lives. That is the essence of Martin Luther King Jr.'s famous citation in his last sermon, on the eve of his murder, when he said, "I have been to the mountaintop." Alluding to Moses, who was allowed to see into but not enter the promised land, Dr. King, almost sensing his own imminent end, declared that short-term trauma was nothing compared with long-term glory. Because for him first things—the kingdom and God's righteousness—were first, nothing could harm him, and nothing else mattered. This was not some mere clever strategy, nor a psychic triumph of mind over matter, but the triumph of the long view, in which human perspective was shaped by God's priorities.

The Long View

Among the chief things that Jesus would have us do is to realize that what appears to be so real, so powerful, so unavoidably worldly, is really only illusory compared to the long-term and permanent interest of God. A person is truly free only when he or she can stand in one world but belong to another, which is why true believers are so annoying to those who are bound by the demands and desires of this world alone. Here, in such a world as this, a believer can be defeated, derided, even destroyed; the alleged winners walk away from the cross on Good Friday having done their worst, and yet, as The Reverend Dr. Anthony Campolo put it, "It's Friday, but Sunday's coming!"

This long view, or sense of perspective and hence of proportion, is what Saint Paul refers to when in Philippians 3:20 he says that "our citizenship is in heaven, and it is from there that we are expecting a Savior, the Lord Jesus Christ." In such a view, according to Paul, the perspective is not passive but transforming for, as Paul further notes in Philippians 3, "He will transform the body of our humiliation that it may be conformed to the body of his glory, by the power that also enables him to make all things subject to himself." This perspective is not that of wishful thinking or of biding one's time; it allows one to endure, to struggle, and to prevail, no matter whether one wins or loses on the world's terms.

If, as Paul says, our citizenship, the place where we really live, is in heaven and not elsewhere, then that is where our loyalties are meant to be placed, first and last. Taking Paul seriously here works when Christian believers are a barely tolerated minority caught up in the persecutions and deprivations of a secular world; when Jews, Greeks, and Romans all regard Christians as not belonging to them, then it is both wonderful and plausible to have a place to which one does belong. It is, however, far more difficult to claim heaven as one's primary citizenship when Christians are running the world in which the Christian happens to be here and now. In this case, heaven becomes a metaphor, but as such it really cannot compete with what is going on on earth.

Perhaps all of this means that Christians who take biblical points of view seriously are not meant to enjoy power or influence in this world. Clearly, the New Testament authors never contemplated a time when the world would take its cues from the Christian sensibility; and when Christians start to run things in this world, they usually do so at a cost to their own integrity. It almost seems that Christians are not meant for worldly power, for whenever they hold it, the claims of a heavenly citizenship seem compromised; there is always the temptation to translate that heavenly citizenship into an earthly domain. The warrant also comes from the Sermon on the Mount and the Lord's Prayer, where Jesus has his disciples pray that the kingdom may come on earth—or be on earth—as it is in heaven, and perhaps this view was most famously iterated by Saint Augustine, noted earlier, when he referred to earth as a "colony of heaven." A Roman citizen and a man of the world, Augustine knew that a colony reflects the salient culture of the mother country but cannot and should not be confused with it. Those who live in colonies work hard to preserve the culture of the mother country, to represent in themselves and those who follow them the culture of the motherland. Of necessity, however, they live where they are, and things are not quite the same as they were. Colonists are caught between mourning the mother country and not taking full advantage of where they are, or of "going native," in the argot of the late British empire, and forgetting the values of the mother country in favor of adapting to the prevailing mores.

It is an uneasy tension, and an understandable one in the days of early Christianity, when Christian values and those of the world were at conspicuous odds. The task of sustaining a unique Christian identity becomes increasingly difficult, however, as Christian culture melds with the prevailing culture and therefore seems to have more, rather than less, interest in making a success of life in this world.

Sometimes success in this process of adaptation comes at a high price. I continue to live in Plymouth, Massachusetts, and I remain fascinated by the story of the Pilgrim fathers and mothers who in 1620 founded our town. I have read much about them and their heroic efforts to establish a colony in which they would be free to worship God and to provide a little worldly security. Reading *Of Plimoth Plantation*, the journal kept by William Bradford, their second and longest-serving governor, we discover that the Pilgrims practiced a form of community in which all goods were held in common for the well-being of the colony. This would not be a strange enterprise, for they would have had before them the example of Christian community as found in the book of Acts in the New Testament, with which they would have been on intimate terms. Sadly, however, "that conceit of Plato," by which Bradford means the social experiment of holding all things in common, failed, and the colony, in order to preserve itself, reverted to a policy of "no work, no eat," thus encouraging a kind of private enterprise that allows the capitalists of the world to claim the Pilgrims and Plymouth Colony among their ancestors.

Nothing sharpens an argument among *Mayflower* descendants more than the charge that their ancestors, the "saints" and "strangers" of the *Mayflower*, were early communists. If we trace our moral virtues as a republic back to the Pilgrims, only to discover that they were communists, albeit unsuccessful ones, we find ourselves on unstable ground. Although Governor Bradford does not exalt the communist model, he does lament the fact that the colony could not afford to live according to the principles of the New Testament church, and thus in his old age Bradford regarded the Plymouth experiment as, if not a failure, at least a disappointment. The great growth and material success of the colony, by then a much enlarged and more complicated place than the little village established after the first landing, suggested to Bradford that success may be too high a price to pay when a godly commonwealth is the goal. Writing toward the close of his life, he said as much:

And thus was this poor church left like an ancient mother, grown old, and forsaken of her children … like a widow left only to trust in God.

For Bradford, the great success of the Puritan migration to Massachusetts from 1630 onward, and the inevitable expansion of the

Plymouth Colony beyond the confines of the original village, with the resultant new towns and new churches that were signs of success in the world's terms, was in some sense a sign of failure. The holy ideal could not be sustained, the ideal yielded to the real, and by 1692, Plymouth was reduced to an administrative subset of greater New England, with its seat in Boston.

"What Would Jesus Do?" remains a problematic question because it implies that it is Jesus' role to enter into our world and become the solution to our problems, when we are meant to live as bravely and as fully in our world and time as Jesus lived in his. We cannot enter into Jesus' world, and it is a presumption, albeit a pious one, to think that he can enter into ours. We have the blessing of his example as conveyed to us by the Gospels and the teaching tradition of the church, an inheritance we treasure. The life of Jesus is his and not ours; we cannot live his life for him, and he cannot live ours for us, and we are, for better or for worse, on our own. Thus we ask with fear and trembling, "What would Jesus have me do?" Jesus does not sit on the board of directors, he is not in the cabinet, he runs neither a laboratory nor a hedge fund, and he doesn't write a weekly opinion column. Unlike Dr. Phil, he does not dispense free advice on television, so it falls to us to try to figure out what we ought to do in our time, with our own skills and problems, based on what we think we know about Jesus.

The Summary of the Law

When my neighbor and friend Julia Child died a few years ago, the newspapers were filled with tributes to her cookery and her eminent good sense, and among the correspondence was an answer she had once given to a question about her religious beliefs. She and I had met on many occasions over the years, and I did not discuss cooking and she did not discuss religion, but the answer about her religious beliefs attributed to her was one of which Jesus would have been proud, one which he himself gave to an impertinent question asked by the religious elite of his day. Mrs. Child said that her creed, such as it was, could be summarized in the words of Jesus: love of God and love of neighbor. Good theology, like a good recipe, does not waste words. "Love of God and love of neighbor" is what the Book of Common Prayer calls the summary of the law: "On these two commandments hang all the law and the prophets."

To those looking for an airtight Jesus-based ethical system, this may seem too simple, or even simplistic, yet of all the things that we might derive from the teachings of Jesus contained in the Gospels, Jesus himself ascribes priority to these two commandments. If we really want to know what Jesus would have us do, we have to take these two commandments as seriously as he did.

The love of God is not just a sentimental obligation but the incorporation of a worldview that we respond to God as God acts toward us. To be created in God's image—a view from Hebrew scripture that is reiterated in the Gospels—is to realize that we have been made worthy by one who is worthy. There is something of the divine, of God, in every one of us. Psalm 19 tells us, "The heavens declare the glory of God; and the firmament sheweth his handiwork," but we too in our own creation declare the glory of God, for we are, again in the words of the psalm, "wonderfully and fearfully made." While the power and imagination of God is never to be denied, it is an article of faith shared by Jews and Christians alike that our very creation, our very being, is an act of love. To love God is to reflect on God the love that brought us into being.

Infants love their parents, particularly their mothers, because even before they are able to articulate their feelings in words they know that love is what they owe to the one whose love brought them into the world. When a baby is born, biology and science and even sociology are present in the room. The newborn is surrounded by all the technology and support systems that our cultures are able to provide, but the most conspicuous element present in the birthing room is love. When I speak with young parents-to-be, I warn them that in the process of birth some harsh words may be exchanged, and that pain for the mother is not metaphorical but real. Recently I was present when a new father commented to his wife, safely delivered of their newborn, "You said some terrible things to me in there." "Did I?" she responded sweetly. The process of procreation was overwhelmed by the moment of birth, and love became the normative condition. In a moment parents are reconciled in joy, and the infant knows by powers unknown to us that love is the response one makes. The child knows that it is loved, and its response is one of love.

When our biblical ancestors tried to understand and explain the relationship they bore to God, the most natural figure for them to employ was not one of power or mere biology, but the relationship of love, and so the first commandment they put into the mind and mouth of God was that we are to love him with all our heart, soul, and mind. Jesus himself says this:

> Thou shalt love the Lord thy God with all thy heart, and with all thy soul, and with all thy mind. This is the first and great commandment.[2]

To love God is one thing, but what is it to love what God loves? This is not as easy as it sounds, for God's love at times seems less discriminating than our own. We tend to love those things and persons agreeable to us, and the notion that God could love things that we cannot is a hard pill to swallow. For most of us, it is reassuring to think that God loves what we love, and hates what we hate, but if "the love of God is broader than the measure of man's mind," as the old hymnist wrote, then our love of God must extend beyond what we alone know and love to embrace all that which God loves as well. If God loves all that he has made—and he has made everyone, not just ourselves, in his own image—then the commandment to love God means that we must love all whom God has made, even those different from ourselves, and disagreeable to us.

The popular evangelist Tony Campolo recently asked a congregation in The Memorial Church if we had prayed for Osama bin Laden. Up to that point he had had the congregation in the palm of his hand, agreeing with his every utterance and hanging on his every word, but then there was an awkward silence, for we have made of Osama bin Laden a demon, and we do not normally pray for demons. "Pray for your enemies," Jesus said, however, and Tony Campolo had reminded us of this commandment. We have no choice.

Praying for our enemies—and not just for their defeat—is one thing, but what about praying for people who are not our enemies but of whom we simply disapprove, people who have done us no harm, people we neither know nor like? This is the hardest part of the ethic of love, but it is at the heart of the first commandment, that of the love for God and all his works.

Jesus is painfully clear on this point. The Gospels are filled with his affection for and association with the outcast, the marginal, the questionable people of society. A key element of Roman Catholic social theology is that Jesus had what is called a "preferential option for the poor." I have preached frequently on this aspect of doing what Jesus would have us do toward those with whom we'd rather not associate, and I find that this is the hardest thing for good people to hear. For Jesus to love the prostitutes, the winebibbers, the tax collectors, and the outcasts of his day is one thing; for us to do so is quite another, and here "What Would Jesus Do?" provides an example we would rather not follow.

One day I asked a congregation to pray for Richard Nixon. If I had done this in Alabama or in what we might now call a red state, most people would have thought me merely patriotic. In liberal Cambridge, Massachusetts, however, it was heresy, and my request was met with stony silence and suppressed hisses. When, early in his career, Billy Graham announced that he would not preach to segregated audiences, many white Christians were profoundly unhappy with him, for who was he to disturb the settled social order with a call to social revolution? When Roman Catholic theologians in Latin America declared that the gospel had to do with liberation from oppressive social conditions, many who argued that poverty and the like were conditions sanctioned by God called these liberationists social dissidents and fomenters of rebellion and revolution; and with a few notable exceptions, their bishops did all they could to suppress such theological interpretations.

If we love God, and all that God loves, then we are obliged to love even the unlovely and the unlovable. To love those who love us and are like us is easy, and we accrue no credit for it, but if we truly intend to act upon what Jesus would have us do, we enter into new and dangerous territory. When Martin Luther King Sr., "Daddy King," as he was known, came to preach in The Memorial Church on the January Sunday set aside to honor his son, after an extended ovation from a capacity congregation he began his sermon with these words: "I have no hate in my heart, for I love God and God loves us all." This remarkable statement came from a man whose son had been murdered, whose wife was killed before his eyes, and whose other son had died terribly before his time: "I have no hate in my heart ..."

Ernest Gordon was a Scottish Presbyterian who suffered horribly at the hands of the Japanese as a prisoner of war during World War II. He survived unspeakable treatment in a prison camp, and at the end of the war came to be the distinguished and beloved chaplain of Princeton University. Dean Gordon became known as the man who could not hate the Japanese, who both in prison and at

Princeton practiced and preached the gospel of reconciliation. Why? Because as a follower of Jesus he knew that love was stronger than hate and death. Generations sat at his feet and wondered how he could have survived the tortures of his imprisonment and emerged with his faith intact. He argued, in essence, that what had kept him going was not the knowledge that God loved him but the fact that he loved God, and that because of that he could not hate. This did not mean that he was heroic or a martyr in the early Christian sense: it meant that he was trying to do what Jesus would have him do.

Transforming Our Neighbors

The summary of the law is not just about love of God. That is the first commandment; "And the second is like unto it: thou shalt love thy neighbor as thyself. On these two commandments hang all the law and the prophets."[3] This summary is introduced when Jesus is asked by a lawyer, "Teacher, what must I do to inherit eternal life?" Jesus asks him if he knows what the law requires, and the lawyer replies with this summary, "Love of God and love of neighbor." Jesus was pleased with his answer and said, "This do, and thou shalt live." In Luke's version of this story we are told that the question was a trick question, and that because the lawyer was not satisfied with the answer, he asked a lawyerly follow-up question: "And who is my neighbor?"[4] Jesus answers with what is to us the familiar parable of the Good Samaritan; and the problem with that for us today is that we have heard it too often and know how it goes, and what to expect.

In our contemporary society, the neighbor is somebody very much like ourselves, bound by the same experiences and expectations, and living in proximity. In America, it has been said, nothing is more sacred than the neighborhood, for that is where, as a rule, "our kind of people" are found. Social troubles arise when neighborhoods, and hence neighbors, cease to be familiar and congenial, and the ties that bind are broken when the affinity of a neighborhood is broken. That is why gated communities, whereby the alien and the stranger are excluded, are so popular in parts of the United States. The greatest risk to social segregation came from the threats that racial integration posed to carefully defined and defended neighborhoods, because being neighbors presupposes mutual obligation. For many people an ideal neighborhood is the type in which we live with our own kind, be it in an urban ghetto or in a suburban enclave. I live at the end of a cul-de-sac in a lovely tree-shaded neighborhood in Plymouth, Massachusetts, and I know who "belongs" and who does not. We are hospitable to, but aware of, if not wary of, strangers.

This notion of neighbor as one's own people, "one of our kind," was the familiar Jewish notion of neighbor encompassed by the commandment in its original Hebrew Bible setting. Doubtless the lawyer knew and understood this, and pressed his point to find out if Jesus shared the "correct" or "orthodox" understanding. He had reason to think that Jesus held a different view, for Jesus' reputation for dealing with people other than "our kind" was already well known, and so the question, if not a trick question, was a test question.

Are our neighbors who we think they are? In our retelling of the parable of the Good Samaritan, we often pay a great deal of attention to the poor behavior of the priest and the Levite, who are usually described as too busy or too ritually pure to have concerned themselves. Princeton Theological Seminary undertook an experiment a number of years ago whereby a person in obvious distress lay on the path leading toward one of the lecture halls. Unbelievably, most people passed him by on their way to class, including some divinity school students heading to a class on the New Testament and the study of the parable of the Good Samaritan.

What makes the Samaritan of the Gospel "good" in comparison to other not-so-good Samaritans is not who he is but what he does. He shows mercy. What he did, he did not out of compulsion, for he was under no legal or ritual obligation; rather, he acted out of compassion or, as we might say today, out of empathy. We know what he did, but sometimes we miss the point. When Margaret Thatcher was Britain's prime minister, she preached a Lenten sermon on this parable in a London church. The City of London is the financial center of England, the equivalent of Wall Street, and at this service in the 1980s, there would have been bankers and financial people who represented the true believers in the mercantile principles of the Tory party. Mrs. Thatcher took as her principal theme the fact that the Good Samaritan provided the funds necessary for the victim's care, and promised to give more if necessary, her point being that nothing is free, somebody has to pay, and the good society is one in which the funds are available, presumably in the private sector.

Margaret Thatcher notwithstanding, this is certainly not the point that Jesus was trying to make. The enterprise here is not a commentary on medical care, or capitalism, or even on mercy and compassion; what happens is that Jesus makes a new and transforming definition of neighbor. Proximity and kinship no longer sufficiently define who the neighbor is, and thus they no longer define those to whom obligations are due. The neighbor is the one who has opportunity to do good to one in need. Various commentaries on this parable give substance to this expanded definition of neighbor, with one, by Arland J. Hultgren, saying that "Whoever has love in his or her heart will know who the neighbor is," and then, "One cannot define one's neighbor; one can only be a neighbor."[5] Jesus takes a definition of neighbor that is understood to be exclusive and, turning it on its head, makes the notion of the neighbor inclusive, even elastic, so that the definition of neighbor knows no limit. Our neighbor is anyone in need who can take the benefit of our compassion; and thus the second commandment, as expounded upon by Jesus and commended by Saint Paul, is as comprehensive as the first. Julia Child's creed, derived from the summary of the law and illustrated by this very familiar parable, is the essence of what Jesus would have us do.

All politics, morality, religion, and law can be found rooted in compassion and love, and the works that proceed from them are all one needs in order to do what Jesus would have us do, and become what Jesus would have us become. Nothing more is necessary; nothing less will do. How all of this reconciles with the conflicting claims of the gospel and the conventional wisdom is the subject of our next section.

— 2 —

The Gospel
and the
Conventional
Wisdom

FIVE

The Gospel and Fear

There's nothing I'm afraid of like scared people.
—Robert Frost

Most of us remember where we were on September 11, 2001, when we learned that the twin World Trade Center towers in New York had been attacked. For many, the first emotion was disbelief—"This cannot be true!" "This cannot be happening!"—followed by fear that not only had death and destruction struck New York, Washington, and Pennsylvania, but that there would be an epidemic of radical violence all across our country. When reality dawned, fear was the emotion of the day, and we discovered our vulnerability. For a short time it was permissible to ask, "Why do they hate us?" which was a valid question, for why would people be willing to give up their lives to attack us? "Who were they?" was an interesting question, but the real question, at least for a while, was, "Who are we?" Soon the introspection, limited as it was, turned to strategies of vengeance, and the only permitted question concerned how we would carry out our revenge, avenge our dead, and restore our honor. When the president of the United States recovered his voice, he emerged as the commander in chief of a new war that we have since come to call the War on Terror, a war on a strategy, not a country, and without limits. In our desire to do something we were willing to do anything, and participation became the language of choice, with "love of country" meaning doing what we were told and asking as few questions as possible.

Before we reached that point, however, many people found themselves returning to the language of religion, with its encouragements and consolations. On the beautiful afternoon of September 11th, 2001, thousands of Harvard students, faculty, administrators, and friends gathered in Harvard Yard to attend a hastily arranged service conducted from the south porch of The Memorial Church. Just a few months earlier, that same vast space had been filled with more than thirty thousand happy souls enjoying the festival rites of commencement. Now, along with the freshmen members of the class of 2005 who were just beginning their college careers, countless other students, staffers, and citizens gathered as the university chaplains, an ecumenical crew representing nearly all the major faith groups, including the Muslim Student Association, tried to make sense of the morning's events. Harvard's new president, Lawrence H. Summers, not yet even installed, was asked to address the crowd, and he did; and while his words were not memorable, his presence and participation were reassuring.

The most profound moment of the simple ceremony, which lasted no more than forty minutes, was the tolling of the bell in the church tower. We were reminded that on its lip was engraved "In memory of voices that are hushed," and we had the sense that we were standing in one of history's dreadful and defining moments. The ceremony was remarkable in its dissimilarity to anything that had preceded it in that place, or in the experience of most of the people there. It was neither a rally nor, in the strictest sense, a service, but as one student reminisced some days later, September 11, 2001, was a time when you did not want to be alone. You wanted to be with lots of other people, and you wanted to invoke as best you could something that was enduring and transcendent. Even President Summers, no religious man and not much given to symbolism or the transcendent, remarked that it was a necessary and moving occasion. It was.

On the Sunday following September 11th, Christian churches across America experienced Easter-morning crowds. Even in these parlous, secular times, when disaster strikes and inexplicable terror is at hand, people naturally turn to religion to help make sense of their confusion. No cleric I know would say that he or she welcomes disaster for the sake of the "box office," as it were, but not one of us denies the valuable sense of, for once, feeling needed even if we really don't quite know what to do. Should the call go out for moral vengeance, the cross and the flag wrapped up together as we sing "Onward, Christian soldiers, marching as to war ...."? Should we call for peace and reconciliation, and a broader understanding of those who are different from ourselves? Or should we perhaps eschew militancy and reconciliation, and speak only of consolation and the healing of our wounded psyches, offering encomia to the dead and empathy to the living? What, if anything, should we say about our country, our communities, our world?

Our national experience of religion was of little help. We had been accustomed to a gospel of prosperity and success, where our politicians routinely invoked "God bless America," and our national expectation was that blessing America was precisely what God was supposed to do. For many people, God seemingly did it, for "the land of the free and the home of the brave" had always perceived itself as the apple of God's eye. The Pilgrim founders of my home-town of Plymouth, Massachusetts, were referred to in the poetry of the early nineteenth century as the "darlings of heaven," and if God was alive anywhere in the world and favored any nation consistently, God was alive in America and favored these United States, or so the thinking went. We understood ourselves to be the new chosen people, a light unto the nations; and our success in the world, our status as the only superpower left standing, our robust economy, and the fact that in the fields that counted we called the shots, all served to assure us that God was on our side. Patriotism was not only a civic duty but a religious one, and the combination of political righteousness, super-sized religion, and material success conspired to make us easy in Zion. We asked God to bless America because we deserved to be blessed; God could not have a more deserving people than ourselves, and the proof of God's blessings was evident for all to see. We had cultivated the notion that faith and success went together like love and marriage, and as The Reverend Ike once famously said, "You can't lose with the stuff I use," by which he meant the gospel of success.

Thus, the most publicly religious nation on earth was horribly unprepared for its religion to deal with the utter devastation of September 11th. If we were as godly as we thought we were, how could God allow such a terrible thing to happen to us? The debacle of the circumstances meant that a cause of the trouble had to be quickly identified, and into that breach stepped two of our most public and predictable preachers, Jerry Falwell and Pat Robertson. They could not blame an absent or capricious God, as their theology was not sophisticated enough to allow it, so in the infamous remarks of the one supported by the other, they proclaimed that God had abandoned America because of its tolerance of abortion rights, homosexual rights, the right to file for divorce, and other deviancies of the modern lifestyle. Presumably, God had allowed the Islamic terrorists of September 11th to succeed in their nefarious enterprise because of the social malefactors who represented a conspicuous falling away from the worldview espoused by Christian fundamentalists and their evangelical spokespersons. The implication was that the above impurities should be purged from the culture, and that if that were done by means and methods yet unspecified but for which terrible precedents existed in world history, all would be well again and the nation would be called back to God and the Bible.

Fortunately, not many people, including most evangelicals, bought this simpleminded scenario, and so the great question remained, What went wrong? Later we would discover that a good deal went wrong, particularly with those government agencies charged with protecting us, and a great deal more would go wrong when the war on terror became as much about resuscitating the political fortunes of the Republican administration and advancing the ideological interests of certain of its leading adherents as it was about bringing terrorists to justice and restoring the peace of the world; but I get ahead of our story.

Where Was God?

On the Sunday following September 11th, even secular editorialists asked the question "Where was God?" The implication was that God was not on duty, for if God had been doing the right thing by God's people, the disasters earlier in the week simply would not have been permitted. The trouble was that the pundits, so profoundly ignorant of the Bible and its history, did not seem to realize that choosing God or being chosen by God provides no immunity from disaster, and even a simple, surface reading in the Bible of the history of the Jews, God's original chosen people, would have been sufficient to remind anyone of that fact. In embracing the seventeenth-century Protestant conceit of America as the new Israel and Americans as the new Jews, we had chosen to become successful Jews, so to speak—that is, Jews without suffering, sorrow, or loss. We appropriated a Jewish identity, but it was stripped of all that made it biblically authentic. God may have had trouble with Israel, and Israel with God, as the prophets consistently point out, but in our reading, God had had no trouble with us and we had had no trouble with God—until now.

There were some of us, however, who thought otherwise. It fell to me to remind my congregation that nothing in the Bible promises us a stress-free existence in this world, and that to confuse worldly success with divine approbation is a dangerous, even idolatrous, enterprise. When ancient Israel tried it, God profoundly disapproved, and showed his displeasure. When Rome tried it, God let it fall. The New Testament Christians, especially those who expected an early and fiery end to this world, seemed to understand that while this world lasted there would always be trouble and difficulty.

As I considered my sermon for what I knew was to be a memorable Sunday filled with anxiety and expectation, I was mindful of the verse from the Gospel of John that is so often read at funeral and memorial services:

These things have I spoken unto you, that in me ye might have peace. In this world ye shall have tribulation; but be of good cheer, I have overcome the world.[1]

How interesting it is to note that in his farewell discourses Jesus does not promise an earthly paradise where everything works out according to plan. He states as a fact that "in this world ye shall have tribulation." In other words, the faithful should expect trouble, anticipate difficulties, and be prepared to cope with disaster; only a fool would confuse this world with the lost world of Eden or the promised world that is to come.

This seemed, though, a rather unpastoral approach to what was clearly a pastoral crisis in the hearts and minds of God's people in

America. Those for whom God never entered the equation presumably were spared the ecclesiastical issues and could confine their angst and anxiety to matters of policy and strategy. Believers, even "unbelieving believers," in that felicitous phrase of B. Davie Napier, were concerned enough to deal with the question of faith in the face of disaster, and therefore I took a different text, one clearly speaking out of the experience of a people who had known the conflict of faith with experience, and the resulting confusion as to how to proceed. The text was this:

> Set a straight course and keep to it; and do not be dismayed in the face of adversity.[2]

It sounds vaguely familiar, although it comes from one of the books in the Apocrypha, and is given here in the Revised English Bible translation. In the King James Version it is even clearer in its sense:

> Set thy heart aright, and constantly endure, and make not haste in time of calamity.

Such a verse seemed to make a good deal of sense in a time when people were losing heart, uncertain of what endurance meant, and tempted in the face of calamity to rush to judgment and action.

When the pundits and editorialists asked, "Where was God?" they meant in part to argue at least one of two points: (1) If we are nice to God, why isn't God nice to us? Isn't that what the bargain is, what he is supposed to do? or (2) All this attention paid to God is wasted if, when we need him most, he isn't there. Isn't this a wake-up call to a mature and secular understanding of how the world works? The question, with its irony and cynicism, was not dissimilar to the contest between Elijah and the priests of Baal in the Hebrew Bible. The God who could deliver fire was the God who was to be taken seriously. The priests of Baal dance and scream and slash themselves, as was their custom, but their god does not show up. The prophet Elijah taunts them and says, "Call him louder," suggesting that he is asleep or, in the delicate translation of the King James Version, that he is on a "private journey," meaning detained in the loo. The Baalim and their god are humiliated, and Elijah and the God of Israel prevail. This whole encounter can be wonderfully experienced in Mendelssohn's oratorio *Elijah*, or one can simply read about it in 1 Kings 18.

The real issue for consideration, however, was how faithful people deal with tribulation in the world, and as the question is not new, we should not be surprised to discover a wide range of answers. Tribulation, the text from Ecclesiasticus 2:2 suggests, goes with the territory, and has done so ever since Adam and Eve were expelled from the Garden of Eden and forbidden to return by fearsome angelic sentries.

Good People and Bad Things

It is a dangerous, even heretical, notion that Christians, even faithful Christians, have a right to expect a turmoil-free existence, that somehow we are entitled to a "Get out of jail free" Monopoly card. We sometimes assume that if only we go to church, or believe in the right things, or do the right things, all will be well.

Where did we get such an idea? When Rabbi Kushner wrote his famous bestseller, *When Bad Things Happen to Good People*, he was tapping into the popular assumption that "good" people are somehow entitled to expect a little favorable reciprocity when bad things happen. This is a profound misreading of the Christian faith, and at the very least it is an incompetent reading of the Bible. What is dangerous about this view of things is that it tends to make an idol of prosperity, and that even if we use religious language in such a view, we are tempted to worship the blessings and not the source of the blessings. From that we soon come to believe that we deserve the blessings, that we have earned them, and that they are a right like life, liberty, and the pursuit of happiness. When we are forcibly reminded that tribulation and adversity are the rule and not the exception, we come to realize, if we are at all realistic, that a gospel of success and a religion of prosperity fail to prepare us to deal with adversity. We are exposed to what Saint Paul calls the "frailty of our own hearts," and that is not a sufficiently strong organ upon which to depend when things are not going our way.

In times of prosperity, when we appear to be in charge, either we make a god of prosperity or we discover that we can do well enough without God or religion, but when we are knocked flat, when what we most value—our sense of security and invulnerability—is taken from us, unless we remember Job, who did not yield to the temptation to curse God even when he had good reason to do so, we will ask, Where is God when we need him to do our bidding?

How easy it is to forget that we worship God not because of what he does for us but because of who he is. The long view, to which we have referred earlier, allows us to remember this. It takes a sturdy faith to remember in the midst of tribulation who God is; such a faith is like a deeply rooted tree that can handle bad weather and neglect. For many Americans, alas, in the days after September 11th, faith proved to be less like a tree and more like a vase of cut flowers, beautiful to behold, magnificent in arrangement, but possessing only a temporary, impermanent beauty. That is why I had us sing Luther's great hymn, "A Mighty Fortress Is Our God," with its tremendous lines:

> *Let goods and kindred go,*
> *This mortal life also;*
> *The body they may kill,*

God's truth abideth still:
His kingdom is forever.

This was strong medicine for tender times, and not everyone appreciated my effort to place terror and faith in context; more than a few people even accused me of the double sin of insensitivity and lack of genuine patriotism. Rather than be reminded of the fallen world in which we live, and of the need for a faith that goes beyond the support of the status quo, my critics wanted reassurance that all was well, that God was on our side, and that in the end all would be in order, which is to say, as it was before this trouble. To say anything less than this was, in the eyes of some of my critics, to challenge either our country and our government, or our faith, and to some the ultimate criticism was that both were challenged at the point where we needed a congenial version of each to sustain us in a dangerous and delicate moment. Surprisingly enough, nobody walked out of church, but I did receive quite a few letters from people who were listening and didn't like what they heard. That reaction suggested to me that I was doing my job.

Inner Strength

What is the inner strength upon which we can call when we find ourselves nearly overwhelmed by outer turmoil? That seemed to me then, as it seems to me now, the question, and not how we should avoid turmoil or where God is when we need him to keep tribulation far from us. Before we turn too quickly to an answer, we must remember one abiding fact, and that is that the world has always been a dangerous and precarious place. This is one reason that the early Christians longed for its end. Their assessment of the future was based upon their realization that things were not likely to get much better—and we know that eschatology, the technical discussion of the end-time and the future it will bring, has been said to disparage the present in favor of a future that never quite makes it. We will speak more of eschatology and the future in a later chapter, but an honest assessment of the present for the believer always suggests that better days are to come and, as W. H. Auden has reminded us, that the "time being" is the most difficult time of all. We can argue for all the improvements made in our lives and world over time; it is a good thing to be living today and not yesterday, because progress has been made in so many ways and in so many lives. The constructive way of looking at this is to say, "But we have not yet arrived at where we are going." The rather negative way of looking at our present state is to say, as I believe the philosopher Alfred North Whitehead once said, "All our progress is but improved means to unimproved ends."

So, if we are to seek guidance for the kind of inner strength that we require to withstand the outer turmoil of which September 11th, 2001, is but a potent part, we should look at how those who suffered in the world before us managed. A pastoral case in point: Some years ago, a very able, attractive young professional in my congregation came to me for counsel. She was having a hard time taking in the grim facts of a terrible medical diagnosis and wanted to know if I could suggest any spiritual reading that might help her as she struggled with God's mercy and her own mortality. She had the medical side of the matter as much under control as possible; it was interior strength that she sought, and she wondered if the Bible could help. My suggestion was that she read through the one hundred and fifty psalms, ideally in one sitting but over not more than two or three days, that she read them without commentary and in an unfamiliar English translation, and that she read them without trying to understand them, but to appropriate them and respond to them as she saw fit. I further asked that when she had finished, she come to see me again.

She did as I asked, and when she returned I asked her how it had gone. Her response was that she had been amazed by the range of emotion and intensity in the psalms: "Whoever wrote them," she said, "had exactly my same sense of ups and downs, exaltation and despair." She felt secure in knowing that somebody else had had the same set of roller-coaster emotions, and that it was all right to feel anger, joy, consolation, frustration, peace, turmoil, and resignation, often at the same time, for they were the emotions of the psalmist and they gave her permission to respond to God and to her circumstances just as the psalmist had. All the psalms she had known before this encounter were quiet and pastoral, such as the Twenty-third Psalm, or praise psalms such as Psalm 100. The others, she discovered, were also written by a real human being who had difficulties with God and lived in a world riddled with unfairness and ambiguity. Somehow the inner strength of the psalmist came through and proved helpful to her.

Reading the psalms did not make her cancer go away—this was not a new form of medical therapy—but it did suggest that others who have suffered have been able to find in and through their suffering a way to God's inner strength whereby the outer turmoil is managed. It may not work that way for everybody, but on her own testimony it was helpful to her. I believe that it is for these reasons that the psalms have long justified their place as the hymnbook of Jews and Christians, for it is in those songs that we find ourselves and the God who is beyond them and ourselves.

In one of his great poems, "Choruses from *The Rock*," T. S. Eliot asks, "Why should men love the Church?" This is his answer:

She tells them of Life and Death, and of all that they would forget.
She is tender where they would be hard, and hard where they like
*   to be soft.*
She tells them of Evil and Sin, and other unpleasant facts.

They constantly try to escape
From the darkness outside and within
By dreaming of systems so perfect that no one will need to be good . . .

"Dreaming of systems so perfect that no one will need to be good" seems an apt description of much of the effort of modern life, even in the church. Somehow, if we can elect the right people, or enact the right program, or secure the right leadership, or provide the right resources, we will reach that point where we can justify who we are and what we have or have not done; and then we can declare, in the words of Mae West, that "goodness has nothing to do with it."

There is, however, no system so perfect that no one will need to be good. Our little systems have their day, and yet even our system of Christian capitalism is inadequate. The rising tide does not lift all boats without putting some people at risk, and because we are not yet good enough to share, we devise reasons why it is somehow God's will that the poor get poorer and the rich get richer. When we are tempted to correct this on the grounds of Christian equality in the political realm, the proponents of change are told not to mix politics with religion unless religion is used to support the status quo of the political order. Goodness has everything to do with it, and I am convinced that not only will there always be outer turmoil, but inner peace will always be compromised until we recognize and affirm that we cannot be ruled by our fears but only by our hopes.

Inner strength comes from the sure conviction that God has placed us in the world to do the work of life, and not of death. What this means socially we will discuss toward the close of this book when the recovery of a social gospel is addressed. What it means for individuals is that inner strength comes not from stoic endurance or even heroic resistance, but from doing what God means us to do in life, despite fear, doubt, and even death. The kind of inner strength that stands the test, even when we wish we were not tested, is best described by Saint Paul in Romans 8:

> For I am persuaded, that neither death, nor life, nor angels, nor principalities, nor powers, nor things present, nor things to come, nor height, nor depth, nor any other creature, shall be able to separate us from the love of God, which is in Christ Jesus our Lord.[3]

Usually we read these verses to remind ourselves that even death cannot break the bond we have with God, but I think it is equally important to remember that death is only one of the things that God's love overcomes. It is that love that allows us not simply to endure but to overcome, when our time of testing comes, and it is the constant assurance that God allows us to be. In his sermon at Washington's National Cathedral on the National Day of Mourning, Billy Graham reminded the grief-stricken nation of this conviction when he quoted George Keith's powerful old hymn, "How Firm a Foundation":

> *Fear not, he is with thee; O be not dismayed!*
> *For he is thy God, and will still give thee aid:*
> *He'll strengthen thee, help thee, and cause thee to stand*
> *Upheld by his righteous, omnipotent hand.*

Most of us retain the image of the firemen, the policemen, and all the other workers engaged in the terrifying enterprise at Ground Zero, and I cannot imagine that any of them asked the pundits' question, "Where was God?" They knew where God was, for he was beside them, within them, enabling them to do the impossible, and not to give up or give in until the task was finished. Certainly, we admired the strength of their hands, but I remain convinced beyond all doubt that it was their inner strength that sustained them and made it possible for them to carry on amid all the turmoil, tragedy, and tribulation in the work that had to be done. Surely God's work had become their own, and God calls us to no task for which he does not supply the means to accomplish it.

Strong Words

In the Book of Common Prayer there is a wonderful collect that begins, "God of all comfort ..." Some people are prepared to stop there, not satisfied with the church's traditional role of offering comfort and consolation when it can do nothing else, but the precise meaning of the word "comfort" is to offer strength, for it has more to do with fortification and being fortified than with consolation or mere sympathy. The inner strength to do what must be done comes from God. The God of all comfort, of all strength, is the one who supplies us with what we most lack when we most need it, and this comfort has to do with power and energy, not simply with solace. The God of all comfort is the one who, in Paul's words, gives us sufficient capacity so that when we are knocked down, we are not knocked out. The God of all comfort is the one who gives inner power and strength to those who would be easily outnumbered, outmaneuvered, and outpowered by the conventional wisdom. Inner strength is required when in the midst of turmoil we do not know what to do with our outward power and might.

In the preceding chapter, I spoke of Dean Ernest Gordon of the Princeton Chapel, and again I refer to his time as a prisoner of war under the Japanese. Dr. Gordon has written that early in their imprisonment the Christians prayed regularly, read their Bibles, and made a great effort to maintain their faith, but that as their conditions worsened, their faith began to waver. Soon, he noted, men turned from the observances of their religion to the care of brethren who were suffering most from the brutality and deprivation of their situation. Dr. Gordon noticed that the men became increasingly responsible for one another, caring for the sick, the dying, and the terrified, and performing among them acts of compassion and sympathy. It was here, not in the formalized religious deeds of their early profession but in the acts of compassion for the weakest among them, that the spark of faith began to glow again, and that the Christian faith was shown to be alive. Some years ago, Canadian pastor and biblical scholar A. Leonard Griffiths pointed out that it was compassion that gave the early Christians their inner strength, and that it was from their inner strength that their compassion for others came, a paradox both intriguing and transforming.

Could it be that compassion is both the source and the manifestation of inner strength? Could it be that what we must do to stand when others around us are falling is to show compassion, to enter into the shoes and the soul of the other? If that is so, how contrary it is to the conventional wisdom of how we deal with turbulent times.

Perhaps the greatest tragedy of September 11th, 2001, and the life we have come to live in its aftermath, is not the loss of the human lives or the buildings, tragic as those losses were and painful as they are to recall. The greatest tragedy may be that we have since been programmed to live by our fears and not by our hopes. Compassion and fear do not go together. Once we were a people defined by our compassions; today we are more and more a people defined by our fears. Political gurus tell us that the party that best plays to our fears and promises to allay them is the party that will prevail at the polls. The election of 2004, we are told, was determined by the so-called values voters. I am not so sure; I think that that election was determined by the masterful massaging of fears.

The Fear Factor

Living in fear is no way for a mature, much less a Christian, society to flourish. Martin Luther feared the peasants whom he had empowered by his translation of the scriptures into the German vernacular, afraid that they would rise up and take power from those who had it. Luther also feared the Jews, lest they change the humiliating terms by which they were compelled to live in the Germany of his time. Thus Luther, the hero of the Reformation and of the liberating power of the word of God, became at once a social reactionary and an anti-Semite for whom compassion was a risky enterprise.

White Christians in the American south feared the black slaves whom some of them genuinely loved, and out of their fear constructed a society based on slavery, which most of them knew in their hearts was incompatible with scripture and the compassion of Jesus. When they lost "The War" and their former slaves were empowered, they lived in terror that vengeance would be wrought against them, and out of fear they constructed a segregated society that was in many ways worse than slavery, because a mockery was made of real and legitimate freedom. That fear was made manifest in the fear directed toward Martin Luther King Jr., until the wiser among the southern whites realized that they had more to fear from others, and even more to fear from Dr. King, if he turned his energies toward the social order and not just to the "Negro problem."

The proponents of national socialism in Germany lived in fear that they would never again control the destiny of their country, and thus it was paranoia and a lust for power that led them to persecute anyone, including Jews, Christians, socialists, homosexuals, and gypsies, who because of their otherness refused to subscribe to a culture based on fear. We all know what price the world paid, and Germany in particular paid, for prosecuting the politics of fear.

Americans lived for a half-century with the fear of communism, worried that it might appeal to disaffected elements of the American culture, or that it would force a redistribution of wealth and power in a way that would destabilize the society as we had come to know it. Neighbors spied on neighbors, and dissent was regarded as the camel's nose to treason. Joseph McCarthy was empowered and long supported by many as he cultivated a climate of fear that came dangerously close to turning the United States into a police state.

The contemporary fear gripping America appears to be a fear of the normalization of homosexuality. What a strange pathology this is—fear that the sexual identity and practices of a minority will somehow taint the identity and practices of the majority. Someone has said that the fear of homosexuals has replaced the fear of communism in American life, and as Americans always seem to need something to fear, homosexuality is an ideal candidate for that role. Gay marriage is seen to threaten heterosexual marriage to such an extent that constitutional amendments must be designed to prevent it, although no one seems prepared to propose similar legislation to prohibit divorce, which is a far greater threat to marriage and the family, and on which subject Jesus himself had distinct views. On homosexuality, he had nothing to say. This irrational fear of the sexual other is all the more dangerous because it conceals itself within the sanctions of religion. Homophobia is the most current example of how good people can end up doing and believing bad things.

The examples could go on. Fear is no policy; it represents the absence of courage and a poverty of imagination. To be defined by our fears is to accept as normal the lowest possible level of emotional intelligence. The risk of indulging in the fear factor is that not only will we not overcome our fears, but we will become dependent upon the means to control and contain them. For example, in our fear of terror and terrorists we are often tempted to resort to the very tactics that we fear and despise in our adversaries. Thus, in Abu Ghraib we engage in torture and humiliation to fight our enemies, making their tactics our own, and in Guantanamo Bay we refuse to apply to the prisoners there, whom we fear, the rights we would expect for ourselves. Thus, how easily we become the prisoners of our own fears and hold hostage our own principles.

Compassion and Strength

The opposite of fear is not courage but compassion. We fear what we do not know, and the mother of fear is ignorance, but we cannot fear that which we love, for, as Jesus tells us, perfect love casts out fear. Compassion leaves no room for fear; we are too busy doing what we can, what we must, and what God wishes us to do, to take time to fear the consequences. If the Good Samaritan had indulged his fears both of the dangers of the highway and of what others might think of his imprudent but compassionate behavior, he would have done nothing at all. Compassion has to do with the exercise of that inner strength that allows us power in the face of powerlessness and of the powers-that-be. In an old commentary on the Beatitudes, I found these helpful words:

> The strength that God gives is available to those who care for others, for they are showing the spirit of Jesus. The power of God's spirit fortifies them.[4]

Can it be that the inner strength of which we speak is not simply endurance, but compassion, not simply the power to bear, but the power to give? The good news that Jesus came to proclaim always calls us beyond the conventional wisdom and into dangerous, uncharted waters. The good news is not "back there somewhere," but out front awaiting us, and there are godly examples of taking that good news as the charter against which we liberate ourselves from our fears. On the cross, from his own inner strength Jesus showed compassion in forgiving his enemies, reuniting his family and friends, and redeeming the criminal. Although he had reason to fear, and there is nothing to suggest that he did not know fear, he was not defined by his fear, and his exercise of compassion, his doing for others, showed the power of his inner strength. As we consider how we ought to manage in a less-than-friendly world, when we wonder on what we may rely, perhaps the answer is found in the exercise of compassion. We should take courage from these words: "The strength that God gives is available for those who care for others." How this works in a conflicted world is the subject of the next chapter.

SIX

The Gospel and Conflict

The race is not to the swift, nor the battle to the strong.
—Ecclesiastes 9:11, KJV

In 1999, a coffee-table book entitled *My Favourite Hymn* was published in England and sold in aid of the British Red Cross.[1] I am certain that it has done well, for the concept is simple: one hundred British celebrities were asked to name their favorite hymn and to tell something of their association with it. Sixty-three hymns made the list, and of those, two hymns that describe the Christian life as a struggle and a battle, in which military metaphors abound, received five votes each, the highest number. The first is John Bunyan's "To Be a Pilgrim," better known in America as "He Who Would Valiant Be," taken from *Pilgrim's Progress*, Bunyan's seventeenth-century book, and versified by the English clergyman Percy Dearmer. It opens with the stirring words:

He who would valiant be 'gainst all disaster,
Let him in constancy follow the Master.

There's no discouragement shall make him once relent
His first avowed intent to be a Pilgrim.

The second verse tells us against what and whom the Pilgrim fights:

Who so beset him round with dismal stories
Do but themselves confound—his strength the more is.
No foes shall stay his might; though he with giants fight,
He will make good his right to be a Pilgrim.

Earlier generations, more familiar than ours with *Pilgrim's Progress*, would have recognized the themes of enterprise, conflict, and courage that describe the Pilgrim's epic journey through the Slough of Despond and other allegorical distractions on his way to the Celestial City. In his travels he fights with giants, or "hobgoblins and foul fiends," as Bunyan calls them, and is tempted and attacked at every point. Life is a struggle, the devil is not just in the details but everywhere, and the only way forward is forward, fighting for every inch of ground and every virtue. In an age in which fighting was what religious people seemed to do all the time and the church was described as the church militant, or the fighting church, such lyrics made sense, and this hymn became the anthem of dissenting Protestants. That it should still prove popular in the late twentieth century is an interesting commentary on the viability of metaphor.

One of the five people who selected the hymn tells why. Frances Lawrence first sang the hymn as a child and was fascinated by its imaginary worlds of hobgoblins and lions, foul fiends and giants, in the original language of Bunyan before Percy Dearmer cleaned it up:

Hobgoblin nor foul fiend can daunt his spirit,
He knows he at the end shall life inherit.
Then fancies fly away, he'll fear not what men say,
He'll labor night and day to be a Pilgrim.

She imagined such a world as far removed from the safety of the church in which she sang, and then, she says, "It was only years later that the murder of my husband brought those fairy-tale images sharply into focus and grounded them in reality." The violence of this world was no metaphor but painfully and existentially real to this woman whose suffering is well known, and whose heroic response to it in the creation of The Philip Lawrence Award toward the advancement of peace and understanding is widely appreciated. She writes, "... we must not listen to skeptics who proclaim that there is nothing to be done. Instead, we must stretch across the streets of violence, fighting not with our fists but with the integrity of the human spirit." No "dismal stories" for her, and she will not fear what men say. "If we have the courage to make this pilgrimage an integral part of our daily lives," she says, "perhaps we shall overcome the vanity of the material world and discover a more sacred destination."

The second hymn to achieve five votes was "Onward, Christian Soldiers," which is perhaps more familiar in America than Bunyan's hymn, although it too is an English hymn, this time from the heart of the nineteenth-century Anglican establishment. It owes much of its popularity to the snappy tune, "Saint Gertrude," composed for it by that master of snappy tunes, Sir Arthur Seymour Sullivan. I always associate it with Salvation Army brass bands, which have an affinity for it, and Sir Arthur used it as the centerpiece of his *Te Deum*, which he composed for the end of the Boer War, but whose first performance, complete with military band, neither he nor Queen Victoria lived to hear.

No less a British establishment figure than Lord Irvine, the Lord Chancellor of England, picked it as his favorite. "The hymns I enjoy most," he writes, "are the uplifting ones." Brought up in the Church of Scotland, Lord Irvine nevertheless has much room in his heart for this most English of all hymns. "I am encouraged by its confident message, whilst it teaches that nothing really worthwhile can be achieved without a struggle: the greater the effort, the more valuable the victory."

The hymn's author, The Reverend Sabine Baring-Gould, wrote the text, as he says, "in great haste," to be sung by the children of his Sunday school as they marched to a neighboring village church. It was meant to be rousing, to give the devil a scare, and to provide some merriment along the road, for people march best when they are singing a song with a strong cadence and words to match. The "foe" consists of Satan's legions, and although "Crowns and thrones may perish, / Kingdoms rise and wane"—a political reality in mid-nineteenth-century England—the children sing:

> *But the Church of Jesus*
> *Constant will remain:*
> *Gates of hell can never*
> *'Gainst that Church prevail;*
> *We have Christ's own promise,*
> *And that cannot fail.*

When, well before the United States entered World War II, President Franklin D. Roosevelt and Prime Minister Winston Churchill held their secret meeting off the North Atlantic coast to discuss what would become America's lend-lease policy, a service was arranged on the deck of the ship and the hymns chosen with great care. Among those selected was "Onward, Christian Soldiers," favored by both the Episcopalian Roosevelt and the Anglican Churchill. FDR's predecessor in the White House, "Uncle Teddy," had run unsuccessfully in 1912 with the memorable campaign slogan of "We stand at Armageddon, and we battle for the Lord," but FDR understood that the war that Mr. Churchill wished him to join was a battle for civilization against an implacable foe. The militancy of Baring-Gould's hymn and the urgency of the times made a perfect match.

It is hard to find anyone today with a good word for "Onward, Christian Soldiers," which has been quietly excised from most mainline hymnals. After Vietnam, the song was shunned because it suggested too much Victorian swagger and seemed to glorify conflict and battle. As did the missionary hymns of the nineteenth century, hymns of conflict, struggle, and conquest seemed out of fashion in a world in which we all wanted to give peace a chance. Only in places where the cross and the flag are likely to keep too intimate company is one likely to hear "Onward, Christian Soldiers" today, and if one wants a rousing, and perhaps bruising, debate, one has only to propose its inclusion in a revised mainline hymnal.

I wonder if we have done ourselves more harm than good by banishing such hymns from our common repertoire. A casual survey of old hymnals of the nineteenth and twentieth centuries will reveal sections of the books devoted to such themes as struggle, conflict, and courage. Here would be found such old chestnuts as "Fight the Good Fight," "Am I a Soldier of the Cross?" "Stand Up, Stand Up for Jesus," "March on, O Soul, with Strength," and that old gospel tub-thumper, "When the Storms of Life Are Raging, Stand by Me." To these would be added "To Be a Pilgrim" and "Onward, Christian Soldiers." Somehow through the singing of these songs we were reminded that life was not a banquet but a battle, that struggle was a worthy enterprise as long as the goal was worthy. The largest Christian youth movement of the late nineteenth and early twentieth centuries was known as Christian Endeavor, and it combined the notions of service and work as the endeavor of a serious Christian. The thrill was that one was working and witnessing against the odds. Struggle and conflict for the right things were ennobling, and glory was found in loyalty to the right cause. Victory, while not necessarily immediate or without great effort, was ultimate, and thus one could die knowing that in the end right would prevail and justice be done.

Victory, however, did not necessarily go to the biggest or the strongest. Faithfulness and perseverance were greater virtues than mere strength of arms, and purity of heart superior to the most winning strategy. One of the best sermons I have ever heard was given many years ago by William Sloane Coffin in The Memorial Church at Harvard. People tend to think of Bill Coffin as a great advocate for social justice, an agitator and an organizer, but some will remember him as a very good preacher. He was preaching on David and Goliath. It takes a lot of work to give freshness to that old story since we all know how it turns out, but Bill caught our attention when he put these words into the mouth of the great giant, clad in all his armor and towering over the little boy: "Hey, kid, whatcha got in the bag?"

Without trying to preach Bill Coffin's sermon for him, I took from his message the notion that mere size was not the determining factor in this or in any other contest, and that an ignorant contempt of that which appears to be inferior and modest can exact a terrible price, as Goliath learned to his cost. Perhaps Bill had in mind Ecclesiastes 9:11, which reads, "I returned and saw under the sun that the race is not to the swift, nor the battle to the strong ... but time and chance happeneth to them all." Here we were, sitting in a celebrity church at Harvard, listening to a celebrity preacher from Yale telling us not to underestimate the power of small things. It was a great preaching moment, and it remains vividly in my mind after all these years, a truth that only grows in power.

The Fashion of Peace

Religion, like the garment industry, has its fashions: themes and modes come and go, and some of us grew up in an era when muscular Christianity and Christian militancy were in vogue. The youth group in my little Baptist church, called the Junior Christian Knights, emphasized Christian chivalry and being good Christians for Jesus' sake, but we boys were drawn to the group by its military imagery of swords, flags, and helmets. Our theme song was the once popular hymn "Follow the Gleam," whose opening line said it all:

To the knights in the days of old . . .

At the evening service in the late 1940s, when taste was suspended in favor of evangelistic enthusiasm, we lustily sang:

A volunteer for Jesus, a soldier true;
Others have enlisted: why not you?
Jesus is the captain, we will never fear;
Will you be enlisted as a volunteer?

We were not singing about fighting in the Cold War, but we understood that war was what Satan waged against the believer and that we believers must fight him back. We could join in Bishop Heber's hymn without blushing:

The Son of God goes forth to war,
A kingly crown to gain;
His blood-red banner streams afar:
Who follows in his train?

Who best can drink his cup of woe,
Triumphant over pain,
Who patient bears his cross below:
He follows in his train.

We could do, or at least try to do, what had to be done because we were neither the first, nor were we alone. Bishop Heber reminded us that we were in good company:

A glorious band, the chosen few
On whom the Spirit came;
Twelve valiant saints, their hope they knew,
And mocked the cross and flame.

They climbed the steep ascent of heaven
Through peril, toil, and pain;
O God, to us may grace be given
To follow in their train.

It seems hard to realize that Christians once sang with such conviction, for to many people today the words sound either hollow or brassy, and many are quick to condemn such sentiments as triumphant and militaristic. The notion of battle and struggle is regarded as unseemly, and Jesus himself, who offered no resistance to those who did him harm, is hardly a poster boy for the church militant.

When Mel Gibson's controversial film *The Passion of the Christ* played in Cambridge, I went to the Ash Wednesday viewing in Harvard Square. The theater was packed to the doors with the curious, and I couldn't help reflecting that it is not on many nights that a theater in a university town can be filled for the showing of a movie about the Bible, in black and white, with dialogue in Aramaic, and no big-name stars. The media had made the film a must-see, however, and I went in the company of a lot of students. At the end, no one moved as the credits rolled. There were some sniffles, but the usual instant and raucous assessment was missing as people moved out into the cold midnight air in silence, no one wanting to break the mood. This being Harvard, however, it was clear that there were many people who didn't know the story and had been seeing a foreign film, as it were. I heard one fellow say to his friend: "Well, he certainly got screwed." I wanted to tell them that this was just about Good Friday, not Easter, but I kept quiet, realizing that those for whom this was the first experience of Jesus and the Christian faith could quite justly conclude that Jesus was hardly an action hero. How could this passive Passion have any impact upon the world?

Conscientious Participation

A former student of mine enlisted in the Marine Corps and did distinguished service in Iraq. In college he was not involved in ROTC, but it was clear even before September 11th, 2001, that he wished to serve his country, and his enrollment in the military was his opportunity to do so. When I think of him, I think of President John F. Kennedy's self-description as an "idealist without illusions," and although I have never asked my young friend what he thinks of this characterization, I think it fits him. This is a fellow who had all the advantages, including a loving, supportive family, the best education that a good preparatory school and an excellent college could provide, and a sense of duty that took him out of himself in search of a higher, more useful purpose. He also attended church and, while not demonstrably pious, took seriously the responsibilities of a thinking Christian. On one of his leaves home from active duty, I asked how his premilitary life had prepared him for what he was encountering daily in Iraq. He spoke neither of carnage nor of discomfort, nor did he opine on the policies or the morality of the war in which he was engaged, but he did say that he felt unprepared by his Christian education to deal as a Christian with the questions of mortal conflict. He was neither a pacifist nor a praise-the-Lord-and-pass-the-ammunition kind of Christian warrior, and if the church had any wisdom on dealing with conflict, he had not heard much about it. As a bright student he knew of the "just war" theory, but that seemed to him like medieval sophistry designed to justify in some rational way wars that ancient Christians intended to fight anyway. He, obviously, was by no means a conscientious objector, but how could a thoughtful Christian be a conscientious participant?

This young man had grown up in a world where peace, or at least the absence of conflict, was the ideal. The struggle to achieve that ideal in a fallen world is not made as clear as it ought to be, and the notion that Christians have always been engaged in a life-and-death struggle for their own souls as well as for the peace of the world is no longer at the forefront of religious teaching. It has long been out of fashion to think of the world as inhabited by hobgoblins and lions, foul fiends and giants; and Satan as an active figure making mischief in the world has been reduced to a Halloween character, or to a particularly obnoxious boss in such films as *The Devil Wears Prada*. The church in many ways has disarmed itself. Perhaps it is atoning for previous excesses of militancy, but the result is that it appears to have no voice when conflict inevitably arises.

This was not always so. Originally, in the Rite of Infant Baptism, now usually referred to as a rite of initiation into the Christian family, the child was not only purged of the stain of original sin and welcomed into the community, but was also armed to fight against a world set implacably against God. The language was self-consciously militant, and after the act of baptism had been performed, the minister said these words:

We receive this child (person) into the congregation of Christ's flock; and do sign him with the sign of the cross, in token that hereafter he shall not be ashamed to confess the faith of Christ crucified, and manfully to fight under his banner, against sin, the world, and the devil; and to continue Christ's faithful soldier and servant unto his life's end.

This is strong stuff, to fight sin, the world, and the devil "manfully"—a word that in these tender days might be rendered as "heroically" or "bravely" to suggest that that quality is not restricted to one gender alone—and as "Christ's faithful soldier and servant" until one's life is over. In the Greek church and in most Eastern Orthodox communions, the symbolism of baptism is made real when the priest strikes the baptized three times with a cross, hard enough to inflict pain so that all may know that the baptized is now prepared to engage in a lifetime of struggle. Somehow we have communicated that baptism is an inoculation against the germ of sin and its consequent troubles, when actually baptism declares that one is now prepared to fight against sin, the world, and the devil. It is no small point to note that immediately after his own baptism by John, Jesus was forced to submit to three excruciating temptations at the hand of the devil. Baptism did not protect him from conflict; it enabled him to engage in conflict and by God's grace to prevail, at least for the time being.

Conflict is an unavoidable part of the world in which the believer must live. The question is not how to avoid conflict but how to engage in it with the least amount of damage, and here the biblical record is not altogether helpful. The common complaint against the Hebrew Bible is that it is filled with violence, for God is described as "angry" and "jealous," and there is no lack of fighting, conquest, and defeat. When the people of God set about rebuilding the broken walls of their city, as described in the book of Nehemiah, in order to defend themselves they do so with instruments of construction in one hand and of war in the other. Jesus in the New Testament says that to manage in this world we should be as wise as serpents and as innocent as doves, but it is also ascribed to Jesus in the Sermon on the Mount, his most important teaching, that the peacemakers are blessed.

Conflict and the Good News

While conflict may be a reality, there is no doubt that peace is the ideal of the gospel. When we read the Beatitudes, where the commendation of peacemakers is found, we make a fatal mistake if we believe that the passage is describing things as they are; and when Matthew 5 is read out in church most people roll their eyes, because they realize that it is not describing any world that exists or ever has existed. In the "real" world, as we know, the kingdom of heaven may belong to the spiritually powerful, but they are cut no slack here. Those who mourn are not happy, and so far the meek have not inherited the earth. Those who suffer persecution are not generally happy, and most of us cannot happily endure slanders and lies. The conventional wisdom tells us that people will at least suffer, and more than likely will be destroyed.

When we read the Beatitudes, however, or, as the Sunday school argot calls them, the "happy attitudes," we realize that the Bible is pointing to something that is yet to be. This is an example of how the Bible points beyond itself to the gospel, the good news wherein we are to be liberated from the burden of the conventional wisdom. This is a visionary ideal as powerful and potent as that in Revelation 21, when after a cosmic struggle with much mayhem and violence, John declares that he sees a new heaven and a new earth.

The first heaven and the first earth disappeared, and the sea vanished. And I saw the Holy City, the new Jerusalem, coming down out of heaven from God, prepared and ready, like a bride dressed to meet her husband. I heard a loud voice speaking from the throne, "Now God's home is with men! He will live with them, and they shall be his people. God himself will be with them, and he will be their God. He will wipe away all tears from their eyes. There will be no more grief, crying, or pain. The old things have disappeared."[2]

Not yet, though, for the first earth and the first heaven have not yet disappeared. This is a vision, an anticipation of things to come, good news for those who suffer under the burden of bad news or the same old news. We will discuss this more fully in the next chapter, which is about the future, but right now we hold out for the vision as the content of the gospel, that toward which the Bible points. We are not there yet, however. We must manage to live in the world as it is until we have the world as it is to be; and a part of this world involves living with conflict. To pretend otherwise is to be unprepared, whereas opportunity, especially for good, comes only to those who are prepared.

Some Things Worth Fighting For

Paul, in giving collegial advice to his young deputy Timothy, says, "Fight the good fight of faith."[3] Certain things are to be avoided, and Paul is quite explicit about them, the allures of which must be resisted and fought against, including vanity, riches, power, the love of all the things that this world values and to which it gives pride of precedence. These are "the vain pomp and glory of the world, with all covetous desires of the same, and the sinful desires of the flesh," the things that the newly baptized are asked to renounce. Paul says, "Shun all of this: aim at righteousness, godliness, faith, love, steadfastness, gentleness. Fight the good fight of faith." These are things worth fighting for, even to the death. They will be in conflict with the values of the world, our culture, even our country, but we are not to let the world's values dominate without a struggle.

Perhaps this is all too biblical? Years ago, I was much encouraged when I discovered that Gandhi had a list of seven social sins that, if not resisted, could destroy both persons and countries. In listing these seven social sins, we find that we are compelled to fight for their opposites in worthy conflict:

- politics without principle

- wealth without work

- commerce without morality

- pleasure without conscience

- education without character

- science without humanity

- worship without sacrifice

We live in a world in which these social sins flourish as much today as they did in Gandhi's time; surely the battle against them is still worth waging.

The Conflict Within

In some sense it is easy to speak of external conflicts: the struggle between ideologies, the clash of cultures, and the like. Perhaps the harder struggles are those that occur within ourselves, between who we think we are and what we think we must be or do or become. I see this often in students, with whom I have worked for more than thirty-five years, who once upon a time came to college unformed and prepared to be remade in some image yet to be discovered. They grew and changed before my eyes, and it was thrilling to watch them discover some new truth, some grand idea, some transforming experience. They came in as one thing and went out as another.

Nowadays, more often than not our students come with some notion of what they ought to be or do, and usually it is something they have done before and are good at. For many such students, college is regarded as merely providing them with the credentials to do what they are good at doing or, at the least, from their point of view, what they ought to be doing. Every once in a while a conflict develops, and one comes to mind in the form of an encounter I had some years ago with a young female student. She was bright, clever, and articulate, and in a fine arts course she had discovered the beauty of Renaissance painting. At one point, filled with the thrill of her new studies, she said that she wanted to go into the art world and become a curator, a student of connoisseurship, because as she had been transformed so she wanted to transform others. Then, as time passed, she got a dose of sobriety and decided to major in economics. She seemed less happy with this new decision, and when I asked her why she had taken such a turn, she replied that she had to be practical. Her parents had worked hard to put her through school and she wanted to pay them back. It was they who thought that economics made sense. She was conflicted between the obligation she felt she owed her parents and the joy of something she had discovered for the first time. Neither of the choices was bad, but she was torn apart by the decision, because choosing between two rights is usually more difficult than choosing between an obvious wrong and an obvious right.

When I was a young instructor at Tuskegee Institute and assisted the college chaplain from time to time on Sunday mornings, I noticed that he always prayed that we would gain the power to choose rightly between the difficult right and the easy wrong. I always thought a better prayer would be that we be enabled to choose between the variations of right that tempted us along the way, and that at the very least we should pray that we not do the right thing for the wrong reason, or the wrong thing for the right reason.

In the book of the prophet Micah are these famous words: "He hath shown you, O man, what is good." What God expects of us is no secret; it is not hidden in an esoteric philosophy requiring a special code to understand it. As my old colleague and teacher Krister Stendahl used to say, "We know what to do." Micah tells us, in the words of the Revised English Bible, to:

- act justly

- love loyalty

- walk humbly with your God

It would seem a simple thing to do. In the law courts of England, before a trial begins it is stated, "Let right be done." To act justly is to do the right thing, to practice the rule that we would act toward others as we would have them act toward us and as God has already acted toward us, with mercy, generosity, and the opportunity of a second chance. To act justly is to do more than the law requires: it is to risk error in favor of goodness.

We practice loyalty when we remember how God has treated us, and when we live and love in the light of that remembrance. We love God because God first loved us. Loyalty requires that we remember that, and because of that remembrance we are kind and good to others.

Humility toward God is perhaps the most difficult part of this activity to carry out successfully, for religious people who are intimate with God tend to be arrogant and lacking in charity toward those they believe to be less intimate with God. When Henry David Thoreau was on his deathbed, his Calvinist aunt asked him, "Are you right with God?" Thoreau replied sweetly, "I wasn't aware that we had quarreled." To walk humbly with God means that we do not walk arrogantly with others.

"He has showed you what is good"—but what about that part of us that, knowing the good, still persists in doing otherwise? Is this not the basis for the inner conflict with which so many of us are afflicted? I have heard many a bright young person say, "I know what the right thing is, I just can't afford to do it" or "I know what the right thing is, I just don't dare to do it." In theology we call this the conflict between the Old Adam and the New Being: just because we may know what is right doesn't make it any easier to do it.

A British Baptist preacher of the nineteenth century, Charles Haddon Spurgeon, who as a matter of course preached to thousands in a year and whose books of sermons were the bestsellers of their day, said:

> There may be persons who can always glide along like a tramcar on wheels without a solitary jerk, but I find that I have a vile nature to contend with, and spiritual life is a struggle with me. I have to fight from day to day with inbred corruption, coldness, deadness, barrenness, and if it were not for my Lord Jesus Christ my heart would be as dry as the heart of the damned.

To some that may sound like too much total depravity, but to many of us it presents a familiar conflict. It is not simply religious self-abnegation; it is recognition of the two natures within us warring for control of our hearts, and hence of our beliefs and our behavior.

When Americans sing "Amazing Grace," which they seem to do now at the drop of a hat, I wonder how many realize that what makes the grace so amazing is its capacity to save us ordinary wretches from our lesser selves. Grace is not praised merely in the abstract. When the former slaver John Newton wrote the hymn, he offered it as a testimony to the grace that had literally saved him and redeemed him from the doom of his life as a trafficker in human chattel. Not everybody will have a transformative experience like John Newton's or Saint Paul's, but we can feel that powerful experience in the hymn, and hope to make it our own. No one knows what interior battles we are waging or how the battle goes, but we can be certain that there is a battle, a struggle, a conflict under way. What a pity we are too clever to be able to sing George Heath's hymn:

My soul be on thy guard, ten thousand foes arise;
The hosts of sin are pressing hard to draw thee from the skies.

O watch and fight and pray; the battle ne'er give o'er;
Renew it boldly every day, and help divine implore.

Ne'er think the vic'try won, nor lay thine armor down;
The work of faith will not be done 'til thou obtain the crown.

Fight on, my soul, till death shall bring thee to thy God;
He'll take thee, at thy parting breath, to his divine abode.

Conflicts of Conscience

How, then, does one live as a conscientious participant in a world that refuses to conform to the vision of the gospel world that is to be, but is not yet? In the weeks leading up to the start of the war in

Iraq, when the president of the United States and nearly all in his administration were busy making the case for war, I found myself on a tour of churches in the heartland of America, giving talks on my book *The Good Life: Truths That Last in Times of Need*. Book tours are hard work but I enjoy them, because I learn a great deal from the reading public. In the question-and-answer sessions, which I take very seriously, I discover what is really on people's minds, which rarely has much to do with what I have just said. Nearly all the questions during that particular tour had to do with how thoughtful American Christians should deal with this upcoming and seemingly inevitable war. They were not the typical antiwar crowd that one might encounter in Cambridge, Massachusetts, nor was theirs a nascent peace movement. They were people who loved their country, took their faith seriously, and were nervous about the state of the world. Everyone wanted to believe that somebody, especially those in power, knew more than they did, and no one wanted to believe that our leaders were uninformed or misinforming us. There was profound discomfort in the land: was there a word from the Lord?

We are all sadder and wiser now, but then it was different, in the days before "Shock and Awe." When I returned to my own pulpit, I preached a sermon that I called "Patriotism Is Not Enough," a title I took from the last words of the once-famous British nurse Edith Cavell, who was executed by the Germans during World War I. The words are engraved on a statue of her that stands prominently above Trafalgar Square in London, just opposite the National Gallery. Her point was that when it comes down to violence between peoples, patriotism is not enough to make sense of it or to justify it. My point was that we should be uncomfortable with a rush to war, even if the conflict is seen as just and easily won. My Christian friends were right to be anxious about our government's claim on our consciences, and perhaps the greatest contribution to what was increasingly a one-sided debate was dissent and an appeal to a better way.

Well, to put it mildly, there were many who didn't quite see it that way, and they did not hesitate to let me know that not only did they disagree, but they questioned my patriotism because I questioned patriotism as the ultimate value of a conscientious Christian. I used the Sermon on the Mount as one of the lessons of the day, which prompted an angry letter from a military man on study-leave at Harvard's John F. Kennedy School of Government. In essence, he said that no sensible person believed "that stuff," that it was bad for morale, and that because of the sacrifice of those who fought without thinking, I was able to utter my seditious thoughts. He hoped that no one had been listening.

I considered my reply carefully, remembering that a "soft answer turneth away wrath." I argued that on balance I was not opposed to conflict and lived very much in the real world where it is a fact of life. Rather, the question always has to be asked in terms of the nature of the conflict, whether it can be avoided, and how it should be managed. The gospel reminds us that it is always contrary to the gospel way to engage in conflict, so that when we do engage in it, it must be with the best information, for the best reasons, and with the sure conviction that engaging in it is less than how we are meant to behave. Mere patriotism suggests that policy trumps principle. If serious Christians are to compromise their principles, of which peacemaking is one, then the policy that bids them do so has to be the best one possible.

Beyond the "Real" World

The reaction to my "Patriotism Is Not Enough," sermon was then, however, and this is now. I think that more and more of us agree that the policy that led us to the war in Iraq was flawed, and its execution even more so. This is not Monday-morning quarterbacking, for many of us, alas not prominently situated, knew then what we know now. Only Senator Robert Byrd, heretofore no hero to me, seemed to understand the moral and constitutional questions, and far too few clergy raised the appropriate tension between what our Christian consciences dictate and our responsible citizenship requires.

The conventional wisdom will always tell us that might makes right, and as Charles I discovered to his peril in dealing with Oliver Cromwell's New Model Army, "There is nothing more dangerous than a Presbyterian fresh off his knees." The sure conviction that the only resolution of conflict is more conflict has put us into such a frame of mind that today we expect nothing but bad news when we read the newspapers, and we are rarely disappointed. Leonard Greene, president of the Institute for SocioEconomic Studies, recently took out a major advertisement in *The New York Times* in which, among other things, he said:

> We have become locked in perpetual conflict. Yet our diverse cultures and religions teach us to honor life and respect the law. We must acknowledge these shared beliefs, heal our common sufferings, and reject the use of violence. Only then can we stand united to ensure that Bin Laden and other outlaws are brought to justice by their peers. Only then can we establish a peaceful and democratic world community.[4]

Is this just another unrealistic plea from someone living isolated from the traumas of the real world? I think not. Greene's first sentences read: "A terrorist killed my son on 9/11. Child-soldiers are killing children." Conflict is the way of the world. The conventional wisdom tells us that there is little we can do about it, yet people of conscience, especially religious people, and most especially Christian people, are compelled by a vision of a world not yet here to deal with the world that is. I remain convinced that it is the vision of the future, an eschatology worthy of the Revelation of John the Divine, that will help us to shape the world as we find it.

Whatever Happened to Sin?

Some years ago, the great clinician and medical sage Karl A. Menninger wrote a little book entitled *Whatever Happened to Sin?* in which he noted that in the modern therapeutic age the concept of sin seems remarkably old-fashioned, so that modern culture has simply banished it from its consciousness. Only preachers of the old school, and perhaps an aunt or two, speak now of sin, and we might wonder whether, in any discussion of the good news, there is room for the consideration of sin.

For some, sin is an annoyance and an inconvenience. In our Sunday morning service at Harvard we still have a Confession of Sin and a Prayer for Pardon early on in the service, on the sound theological liturgical principle that we cannot truly worship God until we have confessed our sins against God and our neighbor. Over the years I have noticed that many students come to our Sunday service a stylish ten minutes after the hour, a habit I assumed they maintained from the academic custom of beginning classes at ten minutes after the hour, until one day I asked a student why he was habitually late. He replied, "Oh, I hate the confession bit, all that beating up on myself, and so I wait until I know that that part is over and we can have church." This may not be an exact replica of our conversation, but in essence that is what he said; the Confession of Sin was "beating up" on himself, and he didn't need it.

This same student was particularly unhappy during Lent, for then we use the old General Confession from the unrevised Book of Common Prayer, which has that memorable phrase from Archbishop Cranmer's sixteenth-century mind: "We have left undone those things which we ought to have done and we have done those things which we ought not to have done, and there is no health in us." When the Book of Common Prayer was revised in 1979, the phrase "and there is no health in us" was removed, together with the description of sinners as "miserable offenders." When I asked my Episcopal friends who were involved in the revisions why these phrases had been removed, I was told that it was for pastoral reasons, that people resented the notion that sin was both inevitable and intolerable and that as a result, without true confession, amendment of life, and the grace of God, they were little more than miserable. When I tried to point out that the state of misery is a result of sin and not a cause of sin, I was told that such a notion was too subtle for most people to grasp, and that grace was more important than sin. I remembered that in the creation story, in Genesis, the serpent is described as "subtle," and it occurred to me that persons not subtle enough to understand the reality of sin and misery were perfect prey for the Subtle One to feast upon.

If sin is simply ignorance, then education will put it to flight. If sin is simply bad behavior, then punishment and rehabilitation will put it right; but if sin is fundamental to the human condition, a fact of who we are, a part, if you will, of our essential DNA, then this may help to explain why the advances in education, penology, and science have failed to stem the essential cussedness of human beings and the persistence of evil in the world. It is this fundamental quality of sin, that which cannot be separated from our humanity, that our theological ancestors referred to as original sin. There is something about being human that, despite our best efforts, makes it easy for us to persist in sin, and it is to this persistent fact that the Jewish and Christian scriptures give testimony. When in Psalm 51 the psalmist writes that "in sin did my mother conceive me," he does not mean—as many have supposed—that the sexual act that results in procreation is itself sinful. He means that the very world in which that act is performed, and into which one is born, is a world saturated with sin. The story of Adam and Eve in the garden—the temptation to disobedience, the apple and the serpent—was an attempt to explain why sin is as old as humankind, and that everyone born of woman is susceptible to the reality of sin. How else can we explain why good people, such as the biblical patriarchs Moses and even David, the "apple of God's eye," are, and are often seen to be from their own lips, sinners? It can be argued that the whole energy of the Bible is an attempt on the part of people who would be good to cope with the reality of the fact that they are not good.

Robert McAfee Brown, in his 1967 book *Patterns of Faith in America Today*, defined sin in this way:

> Sin is not exhausted in describing individual acts which aren't very nice. "Sin" is fundamentally a description of our entire situation, one of separation from God, alienation from him, arising out of our rebellion, our refusal to do his will, our insistence upon following our own wills.

We know what God wants. Remember the famous passage from the book of Micah? "He hath showed you, O man, what is good." We have the Commandments, we have the moral law upon which so much attention is lavished in Hebrew scripture, and we have the teachings of Jesus, which tell us how we are meant to behave. Ignorance really is not the issue, yet sin persists because we persist in our alienation and estrangement from God, in our unwillingness to conform to any standard other than our own. That instinct is so fundamental that for lack of a better term it is called "original," not because the sins are novel or clever, but because on our own we cannot get away from them.

Connoisseurs of the limited range of humor in the life of President Calvin Coolidge will remember the story of Mr. Coolidge recounting to his wife a Sunday sermon she had missed. When the president arrived home, Mrs. Coolidge had inquired what the preacher had spoken about. "Sin," came the laconic reply. "What did he say about it?" she asked. "He was agin' it," answered the president.

Sometimes it is easier to recognize sin in others than in ourselves. Even in churches with a low doctrine of sin, it is always easier to see sin in others than in oneself—which reminds me of a lady I knew with such a high opinion of herself that she said the General Confession "on behalf of others."

Harry Emerson Fosdick, the great modernist preacher of the twentieth century famed for his sermon entitled "Shall the Fundamentalists Win?" and for whom New York's Riverside Church was built, wrote in 1922:

> We do not need artificially to conjure up a sense of sin. All we need to do is to open our eyes to facts. Take one swift glance at the social state of the world today ... that should be sufficient to indicate that this is no foolproof universe automatically progressive but that moral evil is still the central problem of mankind.

Social sin is easy to see: nation making war against nation, the perpetual poverty of the disinherited, the mendacity of nation-states, and the sources of civil discontent that gave rise to the social gospel and, in our own times, to theologies of liberation. Many would describe racism, sexism, and homophobia as social sins, and to that list could be added addictions to drugs, alcohol, and pornography.

At the heart of all these social sins, however, these corporate acts of malfeasance, are human beings for whom the easy wrong is preferable to the difficult right. It is only in the church that that connection is made explicit, which is why the confession of sin, and thus the personal indictment, is all the more difficult to accept.

If sin is fundamental estrangement and separation from God, then the good news is that God does not wish it to be so, and in many and various ways works to intervene in our lives in such a way that we may choose life over death and good over evil. We cannot accept the intervention or make an intelligent choice if we do not acknowledge the reality of that which we seek to overcome. As the great theologian Reinhold Niebuhr put it, "Man is a sinner not because he is finite but because he refuses to admit that he is."[5]

In this life we do not contemplate a world without sin, and as long as we exist there will be sin. Even religious utopian communities recognize that at the heart of their piety and idealized community lies the terrible spectre of substituting their own exaggerated sense of virtue for the grace of God and seeing themselves as perfect when, in order to sustain their vision of perfection, they do wicked things. This is the point that playwright Arthur Miller tried to make in *The Crucible*, his account of the witchcraft hysteria in Salem Village where good people, in order to protect their virtue, did some very bad things. No one today thinks that the hanging and pressing of women deemed witches was good, but those who did such things were convinced that what they did was right. Perhaps this is the point of the old adage that a surplus of vice is superior to a surplus of virtue, because a surplus of virtue is not subject to the constraints of conscience.

Conscience is that little bit of God implanted in us, that part of ourselves made in the image of God that tells us what we know to be true and good, to which, in our better moments, we aspire. "Conscience," according to Jean-Jacques Rousseau, the eighteenth-century French philosopher, "is the voice of the soul, as the passions are the voice of the body. No wonder they often contradict each other." That is a clear picture and it goes far to explain our human dilemma, but conscience is God's gift to us, an act of grace that enables us, despite ourselves, to act the better part, which is the part God wants us to play. Such an act of grace is "amazing," and that is why that notorious old sinner John Newton could repent of his part in the slave trade and write the words that have become perhaps the most famous hymn of modern times: "Amazing grace, how sweet the sound that saved a wretch like me / I once was lost but now am found, was blind, but now I see."

With John Newton we know instinctively that there can be no authentically good news unless we acknowledge the reality of the bad things within and around us, and the grace that allows us to claim the good as our own. When Jesus came preaching good news and the kingdom that was to come, he proclaimed that in the middle of our sin, in the middle of our human misery, we could hear the good news that we are forgiven, and that it is God's will that we receive this grace as God's free gift to us. Of course we sin, but in falling down, and in acknowledging that we have fallen down, we can rise up to try again, and we do this not on our own or by ourselves but because in the proclamation of Jesus we learn, and therefore believe, that God wants us as we are meant to be, and that fulfilling that desire of God is our life's work. It is as Saint Augustine wisely said: "Thou hast made us for thyself, and our hearts are restless until they find their rest in thee." Sin is where we start, but not where we stay, when we consider the good news and the future to which it points.

SEVEN

The Gospel and the Future

Everybody talkin' 'bout Heaven; ain't a-goin' there ...
—Traditional Negro spiritual

The story goes something like this: Two attractive young men in short-sleeved white shirts appear at the door and ask the householder, "Would you like to spend eternity in heaven?" The householder thinks for a minute, then asks, "Will you two be there?" "Oh, most definitely," comes the hearty reply. "Then I don't want to go." The story is apocryphal and cutely antimissionary. Yet, when we ponder the conventional wisdom about the future, it is important to remind ourselves that when Christians consider the future, heaven usually has something to do with it, and the assumption for most of us is that we will be there. For example, lay eulogies these days almost always assume that the deceased, worthy or not, is somehow "up there" and "looking down" in approval or bemusement.

Has God a Future?

New York City's Trinity Institute devoted its 2007 National Theological Conference to the subject of "God's Unfinished Future," which addressed head-on what it described as an American battle over Christianity's vision of God's future. The invitation to the conference stated: "There is a battle over Christianity's vision of God's future. Popular apocalyptic works such as the 'Left Behind' series pit the forces of good and evil in an imminent showdown where God will defeat the forces of evil, the earth will be annihilated, and the 'saved' lifted up." This is a view held by millions of American Christians, and the language of apocalypse and end-of-time conflict is very popular. Televangelists hold forth on the subject, websites proliferate with end-of-time prophecies, and books purporting to explain the signs of the times in this worldview fill the shelves of religious bookstores across the country. The "rapture," a term not found in the Bible and a concept introduced into popular theology only in the nineteenth century, has engaged the imaginations of an enormous number of people for whom current events seem only to confirm the prophecies in the books of Daniel and Revelation. Eschatology, once the sleepy domain of theologians and fringe preachers, now commands center stage among evangelicals and a host of other Christians.

The Rapture

As an experiment, I typed "rapture" into my search engine, and was overwhelmed with documents and citations. For the many who read scripture through the lens of the rapture, there is an almost limitless supply of material with which to construct a theology of it. There is even a journal called *Eschatology Today*, subtitled *The End-Time Review*, designed to serve as "your online revelation guide into the recorded parables, visions, and dreams that make up the Bible's prophetic texts." The journal gives much attention to a correct reading and interpretation of Revelation, a book that for centuries has tempted its readers to try to make sense of times and seasons and to read the current events of whatever age into Saint John the Divine's visions. There is a "Rapture Index," the purpose of which is not to predict the rapture but "to measure the type of activity that could act as a precursor to the rapture." The designers of the Rapture Index think of it, in their own words, as "a Dow Jones Industrial Average of end-time activity." In a mild correction of that metaphor, I suggest that the compilers would do better to think of the index as a "prophetic speedometer." The higher the number, the faster we're moving toward the occurrence of pretribulation rapture.

The online Wikipedia, or Free Encyclopedia, includes this definition:

> The rapture is an event in certain systems of Christian eschatology (the study of the end-times) whereby it is believed that all Christians will be taken from Earth by Jesus Christ into Heaven. Although almost all forms of Christianity believe that those who are "saved" will enter Heaven, the term "rapture" is usually applied specifically to the belief that Christians will be taken into Heaven prior to the Second Coming of Christ, and there will be a period of time when non-Christians will still be left on earth before Christ arrives to set up his earthly kingdom.

The term "rapture" derives from the Latin verb *rapere*, which means "to carry off, abduct, seize, or take forcefully." It was used by Saint Jerome in his Latin Vulgate translation of 1 Thessalonians 4:17. More recently, it was associated with the teachings of John

Nelson Darby and the rise of premillenialism and dispensationalism in late-nineteenth-century America. Darby's theories, always popular, became even better known after they were incorporated into the scholarly apparatus of *The Schofield Reference Bible*, which became the biblical text of record for many evangelical Protestants. Rapture theology has proved to be particularly popular in the United States, where many people believe that America—the new "Promised Land," inhabited by the new chosen people of God—will play a unique role in the end-time. When, some years ago, David Koresh and his encampment were destroyed in the assault at Waco, Texas, Koresh was working on his authoritative interpretation of the book of Revelation, in which he and his people found their place in the end-time narrative. While Koresh's views and actions may be thought by some to be extreme, the view that an end-time time-table can be worked out from the biblical dreams and prophecies, particularly those found in Revelation, is held by a large number of American Christians today, and that conviction affects their views of current events and foreign policy, especially American policy toward Israel and the Middle East. The activities of Russia, the establishment of the European Union, the war in Iraq, and the struggles between Israel and its Arab antagonists all form part of a pattern that, according to such prominent televangelists as Jack Van Impe and John Hagee, to name but two, can be understood only through the correct interpretation of the prophecies of Revelation.

When Is the End Coming?

Predicting the end of the age and the return of Christ has been one of the major preoccupations of Christians since New Testament times; it was expected that after the resurrection Jesus would return, and this time would punish the wicked and reward the faithful. His glorious return, the *parousia*, to use the classical term, would mean the justification, even the vindication, of those who believed in him. The resurrection, as Paul puts it, was not the end of a bad weekend but the "first fruits," the sign of the beginning of a new age. To believe in the resurrection of Jesus was not simply to believe in his personal triumph over death and the grave, but to assert a belief that the long-promised and awaited future, the promised time, was now at an end. Everything in the New Testament is seen through the experience of the resurrection and the anticipation of the second coming, and Hebrew scripture is read and understood through that same lens.

Thus, the great question for the early church was not about the past but about the future, and when the Lord would return. Paul's first letter to the Thessalonians is arguably the oldest book of the New Testament, and in it Paul addresses the oldest questions: When will the Lord come? and what happens to those Christians who die before he comes? From Paul's answer in chapter 5, we know that there must have been debates and disputes about the end-time and the return of the Lord. Given the priority of 1 Thessalonians in Paul's writing, we know that the question of the second coming was a matter of urgent and early concern. Paul writes in 1 Thessalonians 5:1–11:

> About dates and times, my friends, there is no need to write to you, for you yourselves know perfectly well that the day of the Lord comes like a thief in the night.

In other words, the day of the Lord will come when you least expect it, and not on some predictable timetable. All that can be done is to prepare for the unexpected, for just when things appear to be as they have always been, the day will come:

While they are saying, "All is peaceful, all is secure," destruction is upon them, sudden as the pangs that come on a woman in childbirth, and there will be no escape.

As certain and dire as the warning is, Paul's chief concern is how people should live before that time comes. He describes believers as children of the day and not of the night, and he says of them:

But we, who belong to the daylight, must keep sober, armed with the breastplate of faith and love, and the hope of salvation for a helmet.

What is to happen to such people? Paul is reassuring:

God has not destined us for retribution, but for the full attainment of salvation through our Lord Jesus Christ. He died for us so that awake or asleep we might live in company with him.

As a result of this conviction, what are believers to do?

Therefore encourage one another, build one another up, as indeed you do.

Paul is eager that this community of Thessalonian Christians get on with the hard work of being God's faithful people in the world. At no point in his letter does he deny the promise of Christ's return, but it is very clear that he does not want people to panic or, in his own words, to "lose their heads" waiting for the day, meanwhile neglecting all that they can and should do. In 2 Thessalonians 2, he writes:

Now about the coming of the Lord Jesus Christ, when he is to gather us to himself: I beg you, my friends, do not suddenly lose your heads, do not be alarmed by any prophetic utterance, any pronouncement, or any letter purporting to come from us, alleging that the Day of the Lord is already here. Let no one deceive you in any way.[1]

Clearly there had been prophetic utterances and pronouncements, some of them even ascribed to Paul, which suggested the very thing against which he is warning. The day of the Lord's return will be preceded by certain events and phenomena that will mark the signs of the end of the age. Interpreters ever since have attempted to reconcile the events of their own time with these signs of which Paul speaks—and so far, every prediction has been colossally wrong.

Getting It Wrong

Perhaps the most spectacular miscalculation of the Lord's return was made by William Miller, a veteran of the War of 1812 and a farmer in upstate New York who, in 1831, began to preach that the prophecies of the book of Revelation were about to come to pass. He declared that Jesus would come again sometime between March 21, 1843, and March 21, 1844. He was a convincing preacher, and the evangelical fervor of the time made the mood right for great expectations. When the Lord did not appear, however, thousands found themselves disappointed—and dispossessed of their worldly goods, for they had disposed of their material possessions to those who did not share in their convictions regarding the apocalypse. Miller himself was disappointed, but he resolved to revise his calculations and try again, setting a new time of October 22, 1844. It is estimated that nearly one million Millerites shared in his expectations and also in his disappointment, and the failed appointment became known as "The Great Disappointment of 1844." Miller, while disappointed was still not discouraged, and during the month following the Great Disappointment he wrote in a letter to a friend:

> Although I have been twice disappointed, I am not yet cast down or discouraged.... My hope in the coming of Christ is as strong as ever. I have done what after years of sober consideration I felt a solemn duty to do.

Miller died five years later, on December 20, 1849, and his followers divided themselves into a wide variety of doctrinal communities. The Seventh-day Adventists and the Jehovah's Witnesses can be said to be descended from his movement, and in the twentieth century a splinter group of Adventists predicted the second coming for April 22, 1959. This group, also disappointed, further segmented, and one result of the schism within the Davidian Seventh-day Adventists called itself the Branch Davidians, and submitted in later years to the charismatic leadership of David Koresh.

By no means do biblical scholars agree that the rapture can even be considered a biblical doctrine. Dr. John R. W. Stott, for many years minister of London's All Souls Church and one of the leading evangelical thinkers of the twentieth century, refers to so-called rapture teaching as "escapism" and regards it as one of the most damaging doctrines to infiltrate evangelicalism. The Trinity Institute, in the call to its conference on "God's Unfinished Future," wrote:

> The claim of this conference is that this vision [of the rapture] is a massive and dangerous distortion of the biblical picture of

God's purpose. This apocalypticism, in our tradition and others, supports a politics of polarization, violence, and extremism.

A leading critic of the apocalyptic rapture is the German theologian Jürgen Moltmann, whose theology of hope reads the book of Revelation and God's future in a radically different way than most rapture theologies with their scenarios of doom, violence, and exclusivity. Unlike many modern theologians, Moltmann has chosen not to dispense with the notion of eschatology. He does not see it as a fringe element of Christian belief, but as an essential ingredient to the understanding of the Christian community in the world. "From first to last, and not merely in the epilogue," he writes, "Christianity is eschatology, is hope, forward looking and forward moving, and therefore also revolutionizing and transforming the present."

Theology of Hope

Eschatology, with which Moltmann identifies the Christian hope, is not escapism, nor is it fear-mongering, nor is it the anticipation of ultimate revenge. As the great New Testament scholar and poet Amos Niven Wilder pointed out, eschatology is the basis for Christian ethics, for we behave justly in anticipation of a just future. The direction of the faithful believer is forward in anticipation of a place where, in the words of the old spiritual, "The wicked will cease from troublin' and the weary will be at rest / and everyday will be Sunday, by and by." If we read Jesus' Sermon on the Mount and his parables through his eyes, we contemplate an eschatological ethic in which what is now clearly contrary to the conventional wisdom will become the order of the day. The Day of the Lord comes suddenly, but when it comes, it will be a Sabbath, a day when no labor is permitted or required, because all that God desires and all that the faithful seek will be achieved. It will be finished, done, accomplished, and not destroyed but fulfilled, just as it was on the seventh day of creation.

This is a strangely different view of the end of the age from the conventional reading of Revelation or the rapture-ready pundits of the twenty-first century, and a generous God may be a God too generous for the likes of those. In the predictions of doom and violence in which so many appear to delight, there lurks not too subtly beneath the surface a hunger for revenge: "You'll get yours, and we can't wait." The future is a place of terrible retribution, more like something out of a wildly dysfunctional Teutonic imagining than something out of the mind and heart of God. In the minds of those who feel ill-used in this world and less than well regarded, a doomsday future makes perfect sense. In John's revelation we see the logic of one who is suffering enormous persecution and ridicule looking to the day when the tables are turned and the righteous take pleasure in the despair of the wicked. Saint Augustine reminds us, in *The City of God*, that much of the pleasure of the righteous comes from knowing and witnessing the fate of the wicked. They are not only pleased to be saved; they are pleased to watch the unsaved suffer.

Vicarious Thrills

Who is it who does not like to see the wicked "get theirs"? One of the appeals of "professional" wrestling is the notion that the designated villain of the piece, while apparently triumphing through dirty tricks unseen by the referee, will eventually be destroyed by the talent, strength, and justice of his virtuous opponent. One of the reasons I am a keen admirer of Steven Seagal's television movies is that I know his character will always triumph in the end, no matter what horrors and terrors he must endure to get there; and not only will he "win," but in doing so he will punish righteously all of the wicked who until the film's last twenty minutes appeared to prevail. The formula worked in the old television westerns, and in such hero-driven fantasies as *Batman*, *Superman*, and *Spiderman*. Not only do we want virtue to win; we want evil to be punished and to be seen to be punished. Our national infatuation with the death penalty, a cause supported by an embarrassingly large company of Christians, can be ascribed to the same fundamental human desire.

When one combines these fictional heroics with fundamental human desires and with the highly suggestive elements in the book of Revelation, along with a lethal mixture of paranoia and entitlement, one ends up with one of the most popular series of novels ever written, the Left Behind books by Tim LaHaye and Jerry B. Jenkins. These are novels about people who are taken up, that is, raptured, and the chaos that ensues in the world they leave behind. The world will now have to face its various tribulations, and those believers left will have to do battle as "The Tribulation Force," helping to save the lost and prepare for the coming conflict that will consume the world for seven years. The novels represent the kind of virtue-versus-violence that appeals to contemporary fans of science fiction, epochal conflicts, and revenge theater. Add to this the dispensational readings of Revelation, with all the power of Hollywood special effects, and one has a series that cannot fail to please many people. It is to the book of Revelation and the scholarship on it what *The Da Vinci Code* is to the four Gospels and the teaching traditions of the church; but in a world where fantasy is more appealing than fact, such works make their mark. We take them seriously, but not too seriously.

Online, I discovered a document known as "Rapture Letters," which would seem to be a work of fiction but is, I fear, a fact. Noting that the "rapture" means that all those who are born again will be taken up into heaven and that only nonbelievers will be left on earth, the document's creators pose an urgent question: who will tell those who might be interested—family and friends who perhaps spurned advice on the rapture—what has happened and what might happen? The answer is a computer program that will send an electronic message to anyone designated to receive it after the rapture has taken place "and you and I have been taken to heaven." How can this be done? First, it is free, and the hope is that someone who receives one of those letters will get into heaven. The following is from the Web site:

> If you wish to do something now that will help your unbelieving friends and family after the rapture, you need to add those persons' e-mail addresses to our database. Their names will be stored indefinitely and a letter will be sent out to each of them on the first Friday after the rapture. Then they will receive another letter every Friday after that, from "Rapture Letters."

There is a generosity here, but it is nearly overwhelmed by the combination of technology and absurdity. I can't imagine what Saint Paul would think.

Heaven

My late mother, a preacher's daughter, was a very sensible woman, but toward the end of her life she became increasingly worried about heaven. She didn't worry about whether she would go there, for of that she was certain, but she did worry about what would happen there, and one morning over breakfast she asked her clergyman son about it. Her great question was, "What will I do when I get to heaven and meet a lot of the people I couldn't stand on earth? We will be together there forever. What will I do?" I suspect that my mother was not the first person to ask this question, but it was the first time anyone had spoken to me about so practical a concern. In her question she doubted neither the existence of heaven nor her place in it; it was a question of behavior and comfort that concerned her, and so I gave her my best Harvard Divinity School answer. I told her that in heaven we are all changed and become what God has always meant us to be, pleasing to him and hence to each other, and therefore the things that made us irritating on earth would no longer irritate in heaven. It was, I felt, a rather tidy solution. Mother thought about it for a few moments, then said, "Nice try," and remained totally unconvinced.

All the conversations about eschatology, the doctrine of end things and the end-time, and all the details about the rapture and the second coming of Christ, have to do with a notion of the future as both a time and a place. For Christians, the language of that future, that end toward which all of these means point, is the language of heaven.

> *This world is not my home; I'm just a-passing through,*
> *My treasures are laid up somewhere beyond the blue;*
> *The angels beckon me from heaven's open door,*
> *And I can't feel at home in this world any more.*

When in this old gospel song we sing the above, we have joined in a number of assumptions. This world in which we find ourselves is not our ultimate destination; we are, in Paul's words as cited earlier, "citizens of heaven." We belong somewhere else, and our time here is temporary. When people say "Time passes," they really mean that it is we who pass, and that all that is of ultimate value to us is elsewhere, "laid up somewhere beyond the blue," in a place to which we are invited by angels, the permanent residents of heaven. The angels bid us join them, and because we know they are inviting us into a place unlike any other we have known, we "can't feel at home in this world any more." T. S. Eliot puts a similar sentiment in loftier language when he says that the magi, upon their return, were "no longer at ease here, in the old dispensation."[2]

It once was the custom at funerals to pray that the soul of the deceased be spared hell and be forgiven of his or her sins, and at the grave we asked for God's mercy on a sinner because that was the duty of believing family and friends. Today, however, at funerals and especially at memorial services, we all assume that the dead relative or friend has gone directly to heaven and that he or she deserved to do so, that heaven is both influenced and improved by the person's presence. Teary tributes from children and others usually conclude with some variation on the theme, "I know my loved one is up there looking down on us today."

The theme of reunion is vivid in the discourse on heaven. "In the sweet by and by," goes another old gospel song, "we shall meet on that beautiful shore." The Victorians seemed most certain that heaven was the place in which old relationships would be continued and perfected. Henry Alford, a popular clergyman and prolific writer of texts, expresses this view in his once-popular funeral hymn "Ten Thousand Times Ten Thousand," when he has us sing, to John Bacchus Dyke's rousing tune "Alford":

O, then what raptured greetings on Canaan's happy shore,
What knitting severed friendships up where partings are no more;
Then eyes with joy shall sparkle that brimmed with tears of late:
Orphans no longer fatherless, nor widows desolate.

In earlier times, heaven was described as the "New Jerusalem," a reference to the vivid, almost hallucinatory visions of heaven in the book of Revelation, which is where the image of the golden street and harps and bright lights originates. When most people think of heaven, they think of a place furnished more or less as described by Saint John the Divine. Jerusalem, the Garden of Paradise, the Promised Land—all lend their characteristics to what becomes the image of heaven, and it was from those combined figures that Saint Bernard of Cluny drew his twelfth-century hymn of "Jerusalem the Golden" as a place "with milk and honey blest." The visionary demurs at details—"I know not, O, I know not what joys await us there"—and then proceeds to describe them:

> *They stand, those halls of Zion, all jubilant with song,*
> *And bright with many an angel, and all the martyr throng;*
> *That Prince is ever in them, the daylight is serene;*
> *The pastures of the blessed are decked in glorious sheen.*

The clarity of those images of heaven stands in stark contrast to the view of the nineteenth-century American poet John Greenleaf Whittier, whose hymn, now seldom sung, is most appropriate for the postmodern solemnities of death. He begins:

> *I know not what the future hath of marvel or surprise,*
> *Assured alone that life and death God's mercy underlies.*

There is a sense of pious agnosticism here, no claim to superior or secret knowledge except for the knowledge of God's mercy that he is convinced sustained him in life and will not leave him in death. The image that follows is drawn from classical antiquity, the "silent sea" over which the dead were ferried to their final and permanent abode. This journey is neither neutral nor fearful but, rather, benevolent:

> *And so beside the silent sea I wait the muffled oar:*
> *No harm from him can come to me on ocean or on shore.*

Where is the place to which one is conveyed? Whittier is not certain. His journey is like a mystery ride or an adventurous crossing at sea, and it almost doesn't matter, for confidence is placed not so much in the place as in the person who conducts one to that place; it is an exercise in faith:

> *I know not where his islands lift their fronded palms in air:*
> *I only know I cannot drift beyond his love and care.*

Saint Paul reminds those who would tell us all about heaven that we really cannot begin to imagine what it is like. To the Corinthians he writes, "Eye hath not seen, nor ear heard, neither have entered into the heart of man the things which God hath prepared for them that love him."[3] Heaven, the future God has prepared for us, is literally beyond our imagination, and for the time being it is only a thing of the imagination, for no one has gone there and come back to tell about it. When heaven is described in Revelation 22:3–5, it is a work of imagination, a poetic construction, a setting designed for dramatic impact. It is not a photograph, a plan, or a map:

> There shall be no more curse; but the throne of God and of the
> Lamb shall be in it, and his servants shall serve him. And they
> shall see his face; and his name shall be on their foreheads. And
> there shall be no night there; and they need no candle, neither
> light of the sun; for the Lord God giveth them light; and they
> shall reign forever and ever.[4]

Is heaven a place? It is hard not to think of it as such. When the first Soviet astronauts returned from their trip to space, the cynical Soviet press asked them if they had seen heaven. They had no answer; it was a question that literally did not compute. We may smile at the naïve descriptions of heaven that our predecessors provide, and yet, can we, dare we, live without the concept? No less a thinker than C. S. Lewis has written:

> It is since Christians have largely ceased to think of the other world that they have become so ineffective in this. Aim at heaven and you will get earth thrown in; aim at earth and you will get neither.

Earlier Christian generations were said to live in hope of heaven and in fear of hell. What's wrong with that? I have earlier suggested that it is better to be defined by one's hopes than by one's fears, and besides, Jesus spends much more time talking about the kingdom of heaven than he does about hell. Perhaps we should follow the proportions of his thinking. If Georges Tyrell is right that a Christian is a provisional pessimist but an ultimate optimist, then we cope with what we must on earth, living daily in the slough of bad news while sustained by the anticipation of the good news.

John Newton, whose immortality rests on his hymn "Amazing Grace," wrote about the things he expected to find in heaven:

> When I get to heaven, I shall see three wonders there—the first wonder will be to see any people there whom I did not expect to see; the second wonder will be to miss many people whom I did expect to see; and the third and greatest wonder of all will be to find myself there.

There is a charming modesty, delight, surprise, and grace in Newton's description. Those qualities, among others, suggest that the future for Christians is not a place of terror or of fear or of intimidation, but rather a place to be anticipated, for it is filled with grace. It will be the finished new creation of which John Wesley wrote in his great hymn "Love Divine," and it speaks of the generous, loving, gracious God in whose presence is found not fear but joy. If, as the Presbyterian Westminster Confession says, it is the whole duty of humankind to love God and enjoy him forever, then earth is too small a place and our time on it too short a tenure to do that: "forever" is beyond this time and place. Forever is the future, and for believers there is no better word for it than heaven.

Can We Afford a Generous God?

In the future, when all that is to be known about God will be known, when we no longer see, as we do now, only in part, I think many of us will be surprised by the capacious generosity of God. We will, as John Newton said, be surprised to find certain people in heaven if we ourselves are fortunate enough to be there, and we will find that God is far more gracious, generous, and hospitable than we are, that those people for whom we could find neither time nor place are fully accounted for in the joyful presence of God. When I am asked if people who are not Christian get into heaven, and if they can expect a joyful future, I reply with a question: is God just God of the Christian, and is the only way to God the way that we know? Some of my Christian friends are horrified by the notion that God is not a Christian and is God and Lord of everybody, but if God is the author of the universe, God of everything and every-body, then how can anyone say that some people are outside of God's providence? When a Christian says, as a former president of the Southern Baptist Convention once said, that "God does not hear the prayer of Jews," then I know that, at the least, that person has an inadequate doctrine of God. As J. B. Phillips famously said, "Your God is too small." Such a God is parochial, provincial, and unworthy of the praises directed toward him; only God, who does provide for everybody, even in ways unknown or unclear to Chris-tians, is a God who deserves the title "Creator of the World." Just because you and I cannot account for the religions of other people does not mean that the God whom we worship cannot.

Within the teachings of Jesus we have case after case of Jesus pointing to a God who is larger than the conventional wisdom, who is not downsized by the petty pieties of those who would constrain him by their own limited knowledge and experience. In my youth I used to hear of the competing songs from the Methodist and Baptist churches on opposite street corners on a Sunday evening. The Methodists would lustily sing the hymn "Will There Be Any Stars in My Crown?" and the Baptists would sing one of their favorite songs, "No, Not One." Each church thought itself alone, not in the universe but in God's favor, although Jesus constantly points out that God's generosity is greater than ours. How fortunate it is that God is in charge, and not simply Christians.

In Matthew 20, Jesus makes the point of God's generosity in one of his most controversial parables. Whenever I preach on this parable of the workers in the field, with its irritating last verse, "The last shall be first, and the first, last," I sense an almost instant hostility in the congregation. It is a wickedly delicious text to preach in college chapels, where everybody is obsessed with academic rank and position, and to reverse those ranks by making the first last and the last first is to introduce chaos and confusion into what is intended to be a place of order and dependability.

The story, simply put, is that those who arrive late to work are paid exactly the same as those who have worked all day. Those who worked all day did so for a set wage, and because they were faithful and responsible hard workers, and in light of the owner's generosity to the late-coming workers, they not only expected the agreed-upon wage but possibly a bonus. They therefore regarded the owner's treatment as basically unfair, for why should those who did less than they receive exactly what they did? This to them was an act of capriciousness on the owner's part.

Jesus has the owner confront the angry workers as follows: "Am I not allowed to do what I choose with what belongs to me? Or do you begrudge my generosity? So the last shall be first, and the first, last."[5] At first glance this looks like an assertion of power: I am in charge here, the money is mine, the field belongs to me and, for their cost, so too do the workers. "Am I not allowed to do what I choose with what belongs to me?" The rights of the owner are held up for all to see, along with his liberty to exercise his rights. Capitalists find this much totally agreeable.

Then we discover that the parable is really not about power but about generosity. There is perceived in the owner's compensation theory a dangerous profligacy: what will happen in the order of things if people either don't get what they deserve, or, in this case, get more than they deserve?

An English bishop and dear friend of mine not long ago sat for his portrait. Friends said to him, "I hope the artist does you justice," to which the bishop replied, "At my age and at this stage, I ask for mercy, not justice." Strict economic justice may well be what was called for in Jesus' story, but the owner demonstrated generosity and mercy.

Now, when Jesus tells one of these stories it is usually to disturb rather than to console, for those to whom he tells it are the people who think they already know the answer. Jesus, in effect, says to them, "Wait a minute. You do not know the mind of God, you cannot even begin to imagine how the mind of God works with what is his, and since everything is his, everything is subject to the generosity as well as to the judgment and mercy of God." We know this about God, for we have encountered him before. In the book of Micah, we read:

Who is a God like you? You take away guilt, you forgive the sins of the remnant of your people. You do not let your anger rage forever, for to be merciful is your true delight.[6]

Who can forget what it was that drove poor old Jonah to utter desperation? God told him to tell the people of Nineveh to repent, and Jonah said, in essence, "What's the point? They will, you will forgive them, and my prophetic career will be in shambles." The people did repent, and scripture says, "This greatly displeased Jonah":

It is just as I feared, Lord, when I was still in my own country, and it was to forestall this that I tried to escape to Tarshish. I knew that you are a gracious and compassionate God, long-suffering, ever constant, always ready to relent and not inflict punishment. Now, take away my life, Lord; I should be better dead than alive.[7]

Jonah would rather die than allow God's mercy to prevail over his own sense of justice, and while we may despise his attitude, we must applaud the fact that he knew the character of God, and knew it to be greater, more capacious, and more loving than his own.

We should be aware of the dangerous temptation, when speaking of a God larger than our own limited imaginations, to argue that "my God is bigger than your God." I know how tempting it is to use that argument as a clincher in a theological debate, but if we do, we should make the argument about us and not about God. Karl Barth, the great German theologian of the twentieth century, reminds us of not only the greatness of God but also the "otherness" of God, which means that when we presume to speak about God at all we should do so at a distance and with the realization that we cannot speak of God as simply an immense version of ourselves. To do so would be like our attempt, so familiar to contemporary Americans, to communicate with non-English-speaking people by speaking English loudly and slowly, as if by so doing we make them understand. What we know of God we know because we have seen the divine in action in the human Jesus and heard of intimations of God from our predecessors in the faith. When we speak of God we do not speak boastfully or competitively, or in the sense that we know all we need to know, but we can speak hopefully—that is, full of hope—and in faith that the amplitude of God is greater than our capacity to imagine or experience. This is something of which John Calvin speaks when he refers to the sovereignty of God, and it is also what is meant when we speak of the mystery and majesty of God: there is something both elusive and intimate in conceiving of language in which we can dare to think and speak of God at all.

When I think of the future, when I think of heaven, when I think of the end of the age as we know it, I think of the loving, gracious, generous God in whose hands it all rests, and I am glad, even de-lighted, that this God is far more generous than many of his most ardent worshipers and preachers. We Christians, especially those of us who share a Protestant and an evangelical faith, need a bigger God that goes against the conventional wisdom of our little faith. With such a God we need fear nothing the future has to offer, and before that time comes and ends, we might emulate that generosity of God in the conduct of our own affairs, for as that great reformed theologian Matthew Henry wrote, "Our duty as Christians is always to keep heaven in our eye and earth under our feet."

— 3 —

Where Do We Go
from Here?

EIGHT

A Social Gospel

The gospel gives us different priorities from those of the popular culture, and offers us a different agenda from that of the political economy.

—Jim Wallis

One of the invitations I least welcome is an invitation to speak on some college campus in the month of January at a Martin Luther King Jr. Day service. It is not that I lack regard for Martin Luther King Jr. If Protestants had saints he would be one of them, and I am convinced that he saved America from itself and allowed it to begin to live out the full implications of its own demanding creed. I am second to no one in my regard for Dr. King's heroic accomplishments, of which I and all other Americans are beneficiaries. Having said that, however, I still find the day, with its celebrations, problematic. There is a dutifulness about most of those occasions, a sense that "something must be done," and the sad conclusion that inevitably only a black person can do it. In almost all colleges the young people are so far removed from the

civil rights era that Martin Luther King Jr. might as well be a contemporary of Abraham Lincoln. Most black students regard the
holiday as their prize in the social calendar, although there is no
agreement on what should be done with it. Older black Americans
who remember "the movement" wax either nostalgic or angry—
nostalgic for the good old days when race topped the social and
moral agenda, or angry that so little lasting good appears to have
come from those days. Older white people remember when they
played their part in the great struggle and wonder now, in late
middle age, what happened to the movement. Were King and the
movement he personified an aberration, what we thought was a
movement turning out to be only a moment? Is his an impossible
legacy? Has it been betrayed? Mrs. King kept the flame lit by sheer
dint of will, but now that she is gone and her children seemingly
incapable of carrying on the work of their parents, are we left to the
devices of Jesse Jackson and Al Sharpton?

A January Embarrassment

Of all the difficulties attending the observation of Martin Luther
King Jr. Day, the one that nearly breaks my heart is when out of the
spirit of the age we are called upon to sing "We Shall Overcome."
What was once the anthem of the movement doesn't move any
more, and hearing it is like watching Henry Hampton's epochal
television series *Eyes on the Prize* while wondering who those people
were, and realizing how long ago it was and how psychically far
away it all is. The problem is not with the civil rights movement or
even with the song, but that we are reminded of how far removed
we are from those great events, how much remains to be done, and
how little will there is to do it. How naïve it seems now, to imagine
that there was a moment within the lifetimes of many of us today

when it was possible to think of redeeming social sin by moral courage, and to do so under the leadership of a Christian minister who believed that the gospel of Jesus Christ had social, moral, and political implications. Many will, and do, attribute King's moral power to his understanding of Gandhi's principles of nonviolence, but in so doing they fail to recognize that those principles, as well as the legal stratagems of Thurgood Marshall and the public witness of marches, sit-ins, and prayer meetings, were only means to a much larger end.

That end was not only the end of legal discrimination, but nothing less than the bringing of the principles of the kingdom of God into play in the life of America. King was a child of what is called the social gospel, and he felt that it was not good enough to keep the good news locked up in the Bible or restricted to segregated churches, or postponed until the *eschaton*, the end of days. He knew that there was a time when religion and politics in America were meant to be the means whereby America would, in fact as well as in theory, become the shining "city on a hill" of which Jesus spoke and to which John Winthrop referred in 1630 off the coast of Massachusetts. That vision had never been achieved, or at least not fully and for everybody, and this was America's unfinished business. There was a time when we could sing, preach, and pray about radical social justice in church and not be ashamed; there was a time when we could hold all of American society to a common standard of Christian morality that had implications for our economy, our foreign and domestic policy, and the use of our resources and our neighbors. It was on this tradition, the inheritance of a social gospel, that King built, and for a shining moment it seemed to work. Then we moved on to where even the remembrance of such a moment is a mild embarrassment. Before we can move forward, we would be wise to reexamine that inheritance.

A Social Gospel?

One of my most distinguished predecessors at Harvard was a Unitarian clergyman named Francis Greenwood Peabody, third Plummer Professor of Christian Morals and Preacher to the University. He is little remembered now: a grim, modernistic dormitory for married graduate students at Harvard stands as his only monument. In his day, however, which was that period of rapid American expansion from 1880 to 1910, Peabody was famous both at Harvard and beyond, first rising to prominence when in 1886 he persuaded the university to abandon compulsory chapel. It was this act that made him beloved of the students but infamous among more conservative Christians, and it gave rise to the still-familiar epithet "Godless Harvard." Peabody was also widely known for developing courses in which Christian thought was brought to bear on the leading social issues of the day. As the founder of Christian Social Ethics, he discussed such things as social class, alcohol, divorce, war and peace, and the obligations to society of ethically responsible young people. He was famous for his general survey course on Christian Social Ethics, taught not in the Divinity School but in Harvard College, where it was popularly known as "Peabo's Drunks, Drains, and Divorce."

There were many who thought Peabody a radical thorn in the Harvard flesh, but as he was to the establishment born and the brother-in-law of Harvard's redoubtable president Charles William Eliot, he was immune to most criticism. I am not aware that he ever brought his political views into the pulpit of the college chapel, and I cannot believe that he ever endorsed a political candidate from it, but it was widely known that he stood on the progressive side of the political spectrum and was a liberal in his theology. He could be classified among those who believed in what came to be called the social gospel, and he understood, as that movement espoused, that the Christian faith, and Jesus in particular, had more than a little relevance to problems such as social injustice, poverty, and the living conditions of those who suffered at the hands of an unrestrained capitalism. In a place such as Harvard where the privileged were believed to be assembled by right, Peabody stood in the tradition of his abolitionist ancestors, with his preaching and his teaching designed, in words ascribed to Theodore Parker, to "comfort the afflicted and afflict the comfortable."

Although Peabody may have been a singular voice at Harvard, he was not alone in the nation. By the close of the nineteenth century, in many of the larger Protestant Christian churches a full-blown movement was under way to apply the teachings of Jesus to the pressing social questions of the day. Social gospel adherents understood that the "kingdom of God" was not simply some faraway and/or theoretical eschatological enterprise located either in heaven or at the end of the age; it was something to be brought into being in this world by the application of Christian principles to the least in society. The gospel was social in that it was too important to be left alone in the church; it applied to society. A Christian society was not one in which conventional Christians kept out of trouble and worked for conversion and personal redemption, waiting for Jesus eventually to come. A Christian society had a zeal for social reform here and now, it worked for the redemption of the social order, and it manifested itself in its radical critique of the status quo and its determination to make a passive Christian society live out the implications of its Christian profession. A social gospel was the Christian good news applied to the most pressing and conspicuous needs of society.

By the first decade of the twentieth century, the most famous names associated with the social gospel movement were the pastor and teacher Washington Gladden, the theologian and professor Walter Rauschenbusch, and the German biblical theologian Adolf von Harnack. Heirs to this movement at midcentury included the Catholic lay theologian Dorothy Day; Charles Clayton Morrison, longtime editor of *The Christian Century*; and perhaps most famously, Martin Luther King Jr., whose theological education at Crozier Theological Seminary and Boston University was shaped by the social gospel tradition.

Much of the tradition continues in the hymns that were written to extol the ideals of the movement, many of which may still be found in the hymnals of Protestant churches. One of the most memorable is by Washington Gladden (1836–1918):

> *O Master, let me walk with thee*
> *In lowly paths of service free;*
> *Teach me thy secret, help me bear*
> *The strain of toil, the fret of care.*

Here, Jesus is the example, the one with whom we would share in the secret of service, which is also to share in the burden of toil and care. The text is not without its evangelistic sense, for in the second verse there is a call for assistance in the work of persuading others to follow this course of action:

> *Help me the slow of heart to move*
> *By some clear, winning word of love;*
> *Teach me the wayward feet to stay,*
> *And guide them in the homeward way.*

The cause, however, is not easily won; patience is required—what earlier Christian tradition had called the "perseverance of the saints." In verse three, Gladden asks:

Teach me thy patience, still with thee
In closer, dearer company,
In work that keeps faith sweet and strong,
In trust that triumphs over wrong.

Finally, the movement is optimistic, confident of hope's power to shape the future, and the hymn concludes:

In hope that sends a shining ray
Far down the future's broadening way;
In peace that only thou canst give,
With thee, O Master, let me live.

Perhaps one of the most hymnic images of the social gospel is found in Frank Mason North's "Where Cross the Crowded Ways of Life." North was born in 1850 and died in 1935, and therefore lived from the birth of the movement through World War I, the Roaring Twenties, and the Great Depression. He saw America transformed from a more or less homogeneous Protestant society to a place of teeming urban poverty and rural despair. The city, with all its temptations and frustrations, was the laboratory of the gospel, and that is where it was meant to work. After all, the metaphors for the human community in the Bible were all urban, and Saint Augustine's great book was *The City of God*, not *The City of Christian Suburbs*. To this concern, and the sorry condition of the modern city, North writes:

Where cross the crowded ways of life,
Where sound the cries of race and clan,
Above the noise of selfish strife,
We hear thy voice, O Son of man.

With allusions to the city over which Jesus wept, in the second verse North writes:

> *In haunts of wretchedness and need,*
> *On shadowed thresholds dark with fears,*
> *From paths where hide the lures of greed,*
> *We catch the vision of thy tears.*

Jesus himself identifies with the wretchedness of the human condition; there is no condition alien to his compassion:

> *From tender childhood's helplessness,*
> *From woman's grief, man's burdened toil,*
> *From famished souls, from sorrow's stress,*
> *Thy heart has never known recoil.*

Jesus is invited to come down from the mountains, a place of sanctuary and repose, and engage in the gospel work, to "tread the city's streets again," and to do so until human society follows his lead and the city of God will supersede the squalid earthly city:

> *O Master, from the mountainside*
> *Make haste to heal these hearts of pain;*
> *Among these restless throngs abide,*
> *O tread the city's streets again.*

> *Till sons of men shall learn thy love*
> *And follow where thy feet have trod;*
> *Till, glorious from thy heaven above,*
> *Shall come the city of our God.*

The emphasis is corporate, the sins are social, and so is the solution. Saved people will want to see society saved; the two are not in opposition, but one follows the other naturally.

John Haynes Holmes (1879–1964), the New York Unitarian pastor and social reformer, lived to see the social gospel that flourished in his youth decline into the chaos and trauma of what is called, simply, "the Sixties." Holmes, however, fueled by his own powerful sense of social justice, wrote a hymn that could be called the anthem of the social gospel:

> *The voice of God is calling its summons unto men;*
> *As once he spake in Zion, so now he speaks again.*
> *Whom shall I send to succor my people in their need?*
> *Whom shall I send to loose the bonds of shame and greed?*

The text is inspired by the great question in Isaiah 6:8: "Also I heard the Lord, saying, 'Whom shall I send, and who will go for us?' Then said I, 'Here am I; send me.'" It is God, however, and not a willing servant who describes what he hears in terms of the social economy of America in the 1930s:

> *I hear my people crying in cot and mine and slum;*
> *No field or mart is silent, no city street is dumb.*
> *I see my people falling in darkness and despair.*
> *Whom shall I send to shatter the fetters which they bear?*

The answer is to be supplied by persons moved to apply the gospel to the conditions that they see. Instead of to one prophet, like Isaiah, the summons is issued to a community, and it is as a community that we respond. The communal identity of the response is critical, for the work is too great for a single individual no matter how pious or able. Nothing less than a community of right-hearted people is needed for the task of social redemption; nothing less than a movement:

We heed, O Lord, thy summons, and answer, "Here are we!
Send us upon thine errand, Let us thy servants be.
Our strength is dust and ashes, our years a passing hour;
But thou canst use our weakness to magnify thy power."

The sins that prevent our doing the right things are easily named, and to do so is to arm ourselves against them. Thus are the people asked to sing:

From ease and plenty save us, from pride of place absolve;
Purge us of low desire; lift us to high resolve.
Take us and make us holy, teach us thy will and way,
Speak, and behold, we answer! Command, and we obey!

Lest we think this just an American phenomenon, it should be noted that the social gospel began to express itself in England toward the close of Queen Victoria's reign. It has been argued that one of the most remarkable institutional expressions of that early period was the Salvation Army, founded in 1878 by General William Booth. Born in Nottingham in 1829, Booth became a traveling evangelist for the Methodist New Connexion, then in 1859 left the Methodists to start his own movement, which in 1878 became the Salvation Army. His approach was a militant assault on the social evils of the day, and his movement specialized in addressing the needs of the poor and laboring classes. He most famously expressed his creed as follows:

While some weep as they do now, I'll fight; while little children go hungry, I'll fight; while men in prison, in and out, in and out, as they are now, I'll fight; while there is a drunkard left, whilst there is a poor, lost girl upon the streets, while there remains one dark soul without the light of God, I'll fight! I'll fight to the very end!

He did fight, until he died on August 21, 1912, and 150,000 mourners attended his funeral. The poet Vachel Lindsay immortalized him in a poem, "General William Booth Enters into Heaven," in which, among other things, he said:

Booth died blind and still by faith he trod,
Eyes still dazzled by the ways of God.
Booth led boldly, and he looked the chief
Eagle countenance in sharp relief;
Beard a-flying, air of high command
Unabated in that holy land.

General Booth's legacy lives on today in the Salvation Army, whose mission statement reads:

The Salvation Army, an international movement, is an evangelical part of the universal Christian church. Its message is based on the Bible. Its ministry is motivated by the love of God. Its mission is to preach the gospel of Jesus Christ and to meet human need in his name without discrimination.

In its manifesto, the Army says of itself:

I am doing the most good. I feed empty stomachs and hungry souls. I rebuild ruined homes and shattered lives.

At quite the other end of English society was the very well connected Henry Scott Holland (1847–1918), who, as a canon residentiary

of London's Saint Paul's Cathedral, preached regularly to the great
and the good. He was also one of the founders of the Christian
Social Union and served as editor of its magazine, *Commonwealth*.
One of Holland's verses appeared in this magazine in July 1902, at
the beginning of the reign of Edward VII. The coronation of the
new king, the first coronation since that of Queen Victoria more
than sixty years earlier, had dazzled the world with its lavish displays
of imperial pomp and ceremony, but it was to another sovereign
and for another purpose that Holland wrote his verse—which was
quickly turned into a hymn:

> *Judge eternal, throned in splendour,*
> *Lord of lords, and King of kings,*
> *With thy living fire of judgment*
> *Purge this realm of bitter things:*
> *Solace all its wide dominion*
> *With the healing of thy wings.*

The nineteenth century had seen much progress in England, and
the Edwardian age now dawning promised even more, yet there
was something that remained unaccomplished and stood in stark
relief to the signs of progress, power, and wealth:

> *Still the weary folk are pining*
> *For the hour that brings release:*
> *And the city's crowded clangour*
> *Cries aloud for sin to cease;*
> *And the homesteads and the woodlands*
> *Plead in silence for their peace.*

Externally and superficially all seems well, but beneath the gilt of
that gilded age lurked trouble and turmoil which, if not addressed,

presumably by Christian social action, would erupt into the very disorder and chaos of which every Englishman stood in terror:

Crown, O God, thine own endeavour;
Cleave our darkness with thy sword;
Feed the faint and hungry heathen
With the richness of thy word:
Cleanse the body of this empire
Through the glory of the Lord.

These hymns were an attempt to put into words easily memorized and affirmed a social doctrine of the kingdom of God on earth. The movement came out of the realization that material prosperity was not everything and, moreover, that not everyone shared in that prosperity. In part, the social gospel was heir to two profound strains in America's religious past: social reform and personal salvation. In the social gospel movement, however, social reform was the fruit, the harvest, of personal salvation, and personal salvation expressed itself in making a world better for others by means of the gospel.

There was a third element as well, and that was American pragmatism: the social gospel must be seen to do something. It was no good just to preach to the poor, or merely to console them; something must be done to alleviate their condition. The gospel must be applied to the circumstances of everyday life. Thus, in the same period in which the social gospel was beginning to take hold in churches and seminaries, the settlement house movement began with Jane Addams's Hull House in Chicago and soon encompassed hundreds of similar institutions across the nation. The almshouse and the asylum were signs of the problem, not solutions to the social conditions of the day. The issue of poverty was all the more magnified by the existence of the fabulously wealthy in an age of robber barons and no income tax, as well as by the ever-increasing population of urban poor, a consequence of the enormous immigration to urban America. The disparities between great wealth and great poverty in a country that was both prosperous and confessedly Christian presented a moral conundrum that the developing theories of the social gospel were intended to resolve.

Walter Rauschenbusch (1861–1918) is generally described as the "Father of the Social Gospel." A theologian and Baptist preacher, he taught at what is now known as the Colgate Rochester Crozer Divinity School, and in his many books and sermons he gave theological substance to the movement. "We have a social gospel," he wrote; "we need a systematic theology large enough to match it and vital enough to back it." Rauschenbusch understood that a movement for social reform that was grounded merely in guilt or sentimentality would be like a cut flower; lacking roots, it would wither away after a short and beautiful show. Rauschenbusch came along at a period in American Christian life when the choice seemed starkly clear: an oppressive orthodoxy grounded in personal piety and a Bible protected from the acids of modernity, or a modernism in which the values of the scientific method, and the progress of an age in rapid retreat from the claims of orthodoxy, meant that the church would either adapt or, in Darwinian inevitability, die.

I would argue that the social gospel, although related to modernism, offered a third way to thinking believers: here the historic faith, the biblical faith, would be applied in real-world fashion to real-world problems. Who could argue with the mandate "Thy kingdom come, thy will be done on *earth* as it is in heaven"? Presumably, fundamentalists and modernists could agree that Jesus' social mandate for the "least of these" was meant to be tried out here on earth. Surely one could agree that a sign of personal salvation was a willingness to work for the good of the social order. Couldn't one even agree with Rauschenbusch that "It is not a matter of getting individuals into heaven, but of transforming the life on earth into the kingdom of heaven"? Is this not a slight variation on Saint Augustine's notion of earth as a "colony of heaven"?

Fundamentalists and modernists were not bound to agree on much, and the social gospel, rather than serving as a means of holding Christians of differing views together, became so identified with the modernist worldview that it could not survive the stresses of the religious life in a cynical, selfish, and partisan age. The dilemma of "modern man and immoral society," as identified by Reinhold Niebuhr, meant that a social gospel formed in a more optimistic and morally ambitious age could not sustain itself in the face of appealing orthodoxies and private anxieties. With the exception of the civil rights movement, the social gospel went the way of the liberal society that produced it. Has its time come again?

A New Social Gospel?

In the summer of 2006, I found myself participating for the third consecutive season in a discussion of religion in America at the Aspen Institute in Colorado. This time I was on a panel that included Dr. Richard Land, president of the Ethics and Religious Liberty Commission of the Southern Baptist Convention, and Pastor Ted Haggard, founder and then senior pastor of Colorado's twelve-thousand-member New Life Church and then president of the thirty-million-member National Association of Evangelicals. Both of those men were introduced as among the top twenty-five evangelical leaders in America, while I was introduced as a professor at Harvard University. The types were cast: I was prepared to loathe each man, and assumed the feeling was mutual until I talked with them, listened to them, bought and read their books, and thought about the responsibility that falls to those who have great influence and speak where many listen.

By now, nearly everyone has heard of the difficulties into which The Reverend Ted Haggard has fallen. He resigned both his pastorate and his presidency of the National Association of Evangelicals, and admitted to charges of sexual impropriety: homosexuality, which he called his "dark side." Evangelicals were horrified by the public fall and humiliation of one of their brightest lights, and critics of the religious right were pleased to place him in the company of such disgraced preachers as Jimmy Swaggart and Jim Bakker. Having enjoyed his company and been instructed by his books, although our differences, especially on the subject of homosexuality, are profound, I was moved more by compassion than by condemnation. Thus, I was pleased to subscribe to the sentiment of columnist and author Andrew Sullivan as reported in *The Christian Century* of December 26, 2006, where he writes: "I'm praying for Haggard, as I hope he is praying for me and every sinner. But the lesson of this to the religious right surely is 'go and sin no more.' Stop the lies. Stop the bigotry. Deal with the reality of gay people, our souls, our wounded hearts, our humanity, our right to be treated equally by our own government. It's what Jesus did. And it is your true calling now." I suspect that God has not finished with Ted Haggard.

Reading Richard Land's book, *Real Homeland Security*, I came across a passage that surprised me in that I agreed with it. In discussing the sense of the social gospel, Dr. Land wrote, "The idea that there are two Gospels, a social one and a spiritual one, was hatched in the pits of hell. There's only one Gospel, and it's the whole Gospel for whole people."[1] With preacherly hyperbole he made the point often lost upon facile advocates of the social gospel, that the social gospel is the application of the good news to the needs of both persons and society. Social sin does not differ from private sin: both stink in God's nostrils, for both alienate and separate the creation from the Creator. If by "only one gospel" Dr. Land means, however, a gospel that speaks in the terms of individual and private relations with God, then I disagree, and I fear that in his view piety trumps policy. If that is his view, he would not be the first to hold it. Jesus' earliest critics were unhappy with him, and almost cast him off a cliff, because they felt that, in his famously unsuccessful first sermon, in Luke 4:18–19, he unacceptably collapsed piety and policy into a single obligation. Remember that he took as his text from Isaiah the words, "The spirit of the Lord is on me, for he has anointed me to bring the good news to the afflicted. He has sent me to proclaim liberty to captives, sight to the blind, to let the oppressed go free, to proclaim a year of favor from the Lord."

This set of verses, and Jesus' use of them in declaring the start of his ministry, is often called the Social Gospel, and here Jesus does not recognize any distinction between a spiritual gospel and a social gospel. It is all one, good news for everybody, the whole gospel for the whole person, except for those who profit from the status quo, who take pleasure in things as they are, or who are committed to returning to things as they once were. Then, and for them, the gospel becomes bifurcated. They embrace the private part, such as it is, and they shun the public part, for that would be interfering with the divine order of things, which usually means things as they are, or as they appear to be to oneself.

It is not surprising that conservative white southern Christians would resist the social implications of those words of Jesus, for to take them seriously, as a whole and not as a partial gospel, would mean the overturning of the world they had come to know and enjoy. It would mean that society as they knew it was founded upon a lie, and that for the gospel to obtain, their society would have to be overturned and renovated. Change in heart was all right, but change of social custom and convention—well, that was dangerous. It is no surprise that a social gospel with those implications would be stoutly resisted, and it was.

It is not surprising that wealthy capitalists who had struggled by means fair and foul to make their money would resist the notion that their wealth would somehow be redistributed, and that such security as they knew in their world would not secure them against the justice demands of a social gospel. Wealthy men such as John D. Rockefeller and Andrew Carnegie determined that their money would be put to a social good; they understood what Jesus was talking about in his first sermon, and they understood that they were under obligation to do as much good as they could with what they had. Mr. Rockefeller's pastor and adviser, the Baptist preacher Owen Gates, told him that his money would kill him if he didn't find something useful to do with it; and Rockefeller remembered the Sunday school lessons of his youth but, even more, he remembered the social implication of the teachings of Jesus, and he resolved to do all that he could. The best thing he did was to imbue his son, John D. Rockefeller, Jr., with the spirit of philanthropy from which the world has taken great benefit. Had it not been for the moral judgment of the social gospel, however, I doubt that either Rockefeller would have done what he did.

In her book *Jesus Rode a Donkey: Why Republicans Don't Have the Corner on Christ*, Linda Seger was surprised to find that by no means do all Christians agree that the fundamental imperative of the gospel is to help the poor. She writes:

> Although there are more than 2,000 verses in the Bible about the need for individuals and nations to help the poor and the oppressed, there is a powerful group of conservative Republican Christians that does not believe the Bible on this issue. They believe individuals and churches are asked to help the poor, if they so desire, but not nations. They believe charitable giving should only come from those who wish to give.[2]

Seger was surprised to learn that. I was surprised that she was surprised, for it has long been clear to me that people are inclined to approach scripture with an eye to confirming their prescriptural prejudices rather than with the notion that there is something to be learned. It is particularly the case that persons who describe themselves as politically and socially conservative are not likely to look for authoritative sources of destabilization to their status quo, especially when it comes from scripture. The plain reading of scripture, so beloved of those who view the Bible as inerrant, infallible, and inspired, is professed less enthusiastically when it comes to biblical positions that differ from their own interests and practices. For example, in the Bible Jesus has a great deal to say about divorce and nothing at all to say about homosexuality, yet most Bible preachers today avoid any serious discussion of Jesus' views on divorce, whereas homosexuality has become the most divisive subject in the church.

Given the selectivity of biblical values to which many evangelicals subscribe, Seger was also surprised to discover that in 2005 the National Evangelical Conference called for "greater Christian involvement in society, including poverty, human rights, and justice." The National Association of Evangelicals, the body of which Pastor Ted Haggard was president, put out a paper, "For the Health of the Nation: An Evangelical Call to Civic Responsibility," in which evangelicals are asked to address such issues as disaster relief, refugee resettlement, and the fights against AIDS/HIV, human rights abuses, slavery, sexual trafficking, and prison rape. It calls for the "protection and well-being of families and children, of the poor, the sick, the disabled, and the unborn, for the persecuted and oppressed, and of the rest of the created order."[3] This sounds remarkably like a social gospel, although perhaps it sounded too much like a social gospel to some conservatives who would prefer to focus on their tried-and-true issues, abortion and homosexuality, and leave such things as global warming and third-world debt for others to worry about.

Although it took the Southern Baptist Convention nearly a century to apologize for slavery and segregation, the fact that it did so at all, and that its Statement of Faith now calls upon Southern Baptists to oppose racism, as well as every form of greed, selfishness, and vice, is a remarkable comment on the development of a social conscience. The Statement goes on to affirm: "We should work to provide for the orphaned, the needy, the abused, the aged, the helpless, and the sick.... In order to promote these ends Christians should be ready to work with all men of good will in any good cause."[4]

It is encouraging news that the evangelicals are discovering a social aspect of the gospel, if not the old social gospel. Equally interesting to note is that the old social gospel churches today seem to have an ambiguous relationship to their heritage. The conventional wisdom is that the so-called mainline churches were removed to the sidelines because of their priority of the social over the gospel. Thus, churches that were at the forefront of the civil rights and antiwar movements a generation ago lost what the secular world calls market share to those growing evangelical communities that paid more attention to matters of personal salvation and to issues that sustained their worldview. Thus, too, there exists among many old social gospel churches what might be called compassion fatigue, where fewer and fewer people are interested in kingdom-of-God-on-earth issues—and think that the battles are not winnable anyway. Whereas the old social gospel vision was always forward-looking and associated more often than not with progressive politics, the movement now tends to be nostalgic, hearkening back to former glory. The old social gospel is a bit like a Martin Luther King Jr. Day service, warm with memory but frustrated in hope.

For many for whom the Lord's Prayer still envisions God's kingdom on earth as it is in heaven, the temptation has been great to imitate the successful strategies of the evangelical movement in an attempt to recover the gospel side of the equation, and that is not entirely bad. A consistent critique of the sidelined mainline churches is that they were all too ready to substitute *The New York Times* and the latest policy journal for the Bible. In leaving the Bible to the so-called Bible churches, Bible colleges, Bible radio stations, and Bible-thumping televangelists, those churches lost the content that made the old social gospel a religious, and not merely a social, enterprise. In giving up piety, personal salvation, and what the reformers once called the "full wealth of conviction," they dreamed of and hoped to devise, again in the words of T. S. Eliot, "systems so perfect that no one need ever be good." Even good liberals abandoned Jimmy Carter because he seemed to many to be "too religious," for he actually read his Bible, and he taught Sunday school even while he was president.

Jimmy Carter and I once appeared on the same platform at Duke University, where we were being awarded honorary degrees, he as the Commencement speaker and I as the Baccalaureate preacher. He was publicly lauded as one of the great men of our time, received ovation after ovation, and was crushed by well-wishers. He seemed mildly embarrassed by the fuss, and when I said to him that he deserved all of it and how proud we all were of him and his example, he replied, somewhat ruefully, that if all the people who loved him now had voted for him then, he would have won reelection. He was probably right. Here is a man who had a clear aptitude for politics and public service and never lost his soul. He was a conspicuous and consistent Christian in public life, compassionate and competent at the same time and living out the implications of his Christian faith. He was perhaps the last president for whom the social gospel was, in Richard Land's felicitous phrase, "the whole gospel for whole people." For secular Americans he was perhaps too religious, and for the more aggressive evangelicals he was not religious enough, or at least not after their fashion. They preferred Ronald Reagan, whose religious views, if any, were concealed behind his personal charisma and public policies, and now George W. Bush, who, as a recovered alcoholic and a confessed born-again Christian, regards the more militant evangelicals as his base in much the same way that old-school Democrats regarded the labor movement as theirs.

The old social gospel was born in a period of cultural optimism on the part of those Christians who believed that with conviction and compassion the kingdom of God could be ushered in. "Peace in our time" was to many a realistic goal. World War I ran on the notion, at least in America, that the world could be made safe for democracy, and that it was the war to end all wars. *The Christian Century* magazine was founded on the naïve notion that the twentieth century would be the Christian century in which, at last, the principles of an enlightened and applied faith would make the kingdom of God on earth a reality. After the horrors of World War II, the realization of the facts of the Holocaust, and the inauguration of the nuclear age, the United Nations was conceived as the instrument that would supersede national ambitions and thereby make the world a safer, even happier, place. For many Christians this was a work too important to be left to the churches alone, although, to address similar issues within an ecumenical context, the World Council of Churches was founded at about the same time.

Indeed, the ecumenical movement was organized as an effort to overcome the limitations of denominationalism and parochialism in pursuit of Christ's vision that "they all may be one." The social gospel was now to be translated to a world stage. When the old Federal Council of Churches morphed into the National Council of Churches shortly after World War II, it was composed largely of

Protestant churches, many of which had an affinity for the old social gospel but for whom there yet remained a wide diversity of opinion on how Christian ideals should be applied to social policy.

On the occasion of its fiftieth anniversary, I attended an assembly of the National Council of Churches. The large auditorium was filled with pictures of the original gathering fifty years earlier, the room then obviously packed with enthusiastic delegates. Fifty years later, the room was half-empty and most of the delegates were, as we say in Boston, "of a certain age." The contrast between the founding day and the present day was made even more clear by a program in which representatives of churches and traditions not present in 1947 were invited to speak to the assembly. Those speakers represented the Roman Catholic church, eastern Orthodoxy, many evangelical traditions, the Pentecostal churches, and many historically black denominations. Those who had not been present at the founding represented a range of Christian influence far more inclusive and representative than those who had formed the Council, and it was clear that the religious demographics had changed significantly. As recently as in 1975, the Council had been defined by its critics as essentially a lobby for left-wing politics. For example, in his book *Unholy Alliance: The History of the National Council of Churches*, C. Gregg Singer argued that the Council was little more than a mobilizing organization for what he called "the establishment left," and in his subtitle he left little doubt as to his point of view: *The Definitive History of the National Council of Churches and Its Leftist Politics*. The Council's calls for peace and economic justice, and its apparent collusion in left-wing politics, made it increasingly an anachronism in a world where non-Council churches either remained aloof from politics or increasingly associated themselves with the growing conservative movement.

As a counterpoint to the Federal Council of Churches, the National Association of Evangelicals was formed in 1942, representing the interests of "the unvoiced multitudes," in the famous words of Harold John Ockenga, minister of Boston's historic evangelical citadel, the Park Street Church. The National Association of Evangelicals is the institution of thirty million souls over which Pastor Ted Haggard of Colorado once presided.

Hope of the World

In 1954 the distinguished Methodist laywoman Georgia Harkness wrote a hymn in the spirit of the social gospel and of the Methodist tradition of Christian service. In her hymn, alas not now sung very often even among Methodists, she speaks to a world trapped in its fears and between the twin perils of materialism and modernity. This was no longer the world of Washington Gladden, Walter Rauschenbusch, or Francis Greenwood Peabody; she was writing in the context of a pervasive Cold War, a fear of world-dominating communism, and the very real possibility of nuclear destruction. The civil rights movement was in its earliest stages, and all the progressive ambitions that had seemed so achievable in the immediate aftermath of World War II, the so-called good war, now appeared to be held hostage to the climate of fear and anxiety. Could we ever again sing her hymn without wincing?

> *Hope of the world, thou Christ of great compassion,*
> *Speak to our fearful hearts by conflict rent;*
> *Save us, thy people, from consuming passion,*
> *Who by our own false hopes and aims are spent.*

The words are found in a collection entitled *Eleven Ecumenical Hymns*, the copyright of which is owned by the Hymn Society of America, which commissioned them for use in the churches connected with the ecumenical movement. There is a sense of frustration in this text, with our false hopes and aims appearing to have the upper hand. Harkness continues:

> *Hope of the world, God's gift from highest heaven,*
> *Bringing to hungry souls the bread of life,*
> *Still let thy spirit unto us be given*
> *To heal earth's wounds and end her bitter strife.*

She ends with an affirmation of the lordship of Christ and an invitation to be faithful to the glorious gospel. It is not a summons to a new endeavor but a call to renewal tinged by the realities of a world sadder and, one hopes, wiser for its misadventures and missed opportunities:

> *Hope of the world, O Christ, o'er death victorious,*
> *Who by this sign didst conquer grief and pain;*
> *We would be faithful to thy gospel glorious:*
> *Thou art our Lord! Thou dost forever reign.*

This hymn was not in the Baptist hymnbooks of my youth; it was only during my stint as an organist in a Methodist church that I discovered it. Might it be a sign of things to come? Could Christ, the hope of the world, overcome the disastrous battles waged not by his enemies but by those who would call themselves his friends?

Is it possible that after a century of bitter infighting between liberal and conservative Christians in America, during which time cultural power has shifted from a liberal establishment to those "unvoiced multitudes" who are radically empowered, a newly defined social gospel might be the means of addressing the fundamental moral and values issues of our day that neither side on its own appears capable of resolving? Given that our world today is less safe than it was a half-century ago, that the disparities between the rich and the poor increase rather than lessen, and that Christians fight with one another for power and influence while the culture seems to deteriorate, is it possible to imagine a country in which those who claim to be followers of Jesus Christ and devoted to his mission, as found in his first, controversial sermon, can unite in a social wisdom that goes beyond the Bible and into the whole gospel for the whole person?

That remains to be seen, but it is the great question that any sincere Christian must address as the twenty-first century of the Christian era unfolds. In the concluding chapters we will look at an inclusive gospel, and then at a hopeful gospel.

NINE

An Inclusive Gospel

Of a truth I perceive that God is no respecter of persons.
—Acts 10:34, KJV

A few years ago I had the great pleasure of preaching on the occasion of the one hundred fiftieth anniversary of an Episcopal church in Virginia. It was on a splendid day filled with all of the glories that an anniversary can conjure, especially in a place where the past is always present. It was agreed that the service would be of the kind the parish would have known at the time of its foundation, and hence Morning Prayer was read according to the Book of Common Prayer of 1789. As would have been the custom in those days, we said the Litany, or General Supplication, which begins:

O God, the Father of Heaven, have mercy upon us, miserable sinners ...

The people reply in the same words in answer to the priest, and it goes on for many pages in that vein of humiliating petition, an altogether healthy exercise for people who think too highly of themselves and are more accustomed to therapeutic worship: I can see why the more modern liturgies are more popular.

Among the many other petitions was one that particularly captured both my attention and my imagination as I found myself on my knees praying into the bishop's chair:

> Remember not, Lord, our offenses, nor the offenses of our forefathers ...

What an interesting concept it is, to ask God not only to forget our sins but to forget those of our ancestors as well. To this was added the entreaty:

> Neither take Thou vengeance for our sins; spare us, good Lord, spare Thy people, whom Thou hast redeemed.

Here we are in Virginia, I reminded myself, in a church established just a few years before the Civil War and near some of the fiercest fighting of that war. Here is a church where one hundred and fifty years ago neither the current rector—a woman—nor the guest preacher—an African American—would have been allowed anywhere near where we were on that anniversary Sunday. Enshrined in the place of honor in the chancel window over the altar was the figure of George Washington, a Virginian and an Episcopalian, and it was not difficult to remember who the forefathers and foremothers were in this place, nor to imagine at least one of their conspicuous sins, the belief that it was not wrong for Christians to hold other human beings, even fellow Christians, in chattel bondage. I was reminded of the fact that when the parishioners here prayed the Litany or General Supplication so long ago, they were literally praying for their ancestors and not for mine. Thus, I took a small perverse pleasure in praying both for their ancestors and for mine in asking God not to remember past offenses nor to hold them against us today.

The point of the liturgy was that we should not be burdened by the sins of the past, as there is enough trouble today without adding the troubles of yesterday. When, however, we are forced to remember liturgically, as the old Litany requires, we are reminded perhaps more than we would like that more often than not our ancestors got it wrong, and that being religious, or even Christian, did not spare them the errors of their day. While we ask that God not hold their sins against them, and we pray that others will pray the same prayer for us when we have joined our own ancestors, we should be reminded with a painful poignancy that we too can, and often do, get it wrong. That is why the most profound of all religious sentiments should not be certainty, which inevitably leads to arrogance, but modesty, which, because of a generous God, leads to mercy and forgiveness.

The Pain of Remembrance

The remembrance of Christian ignorance and arrogance is painful. In earlier writings I called anti-Semitism the Christian "original" sin, perhaps playing fast and loose with the doctrinal history drawn from the account in Genesis of human disobedience. Although it is true that Jewish Christians in the time of Saint Paul were persuaded that Gentiles had to be circumcised, that is, made liturgically Jewish, in order to become followers of Jesus, and thus were very hard on Gentiles who refused first to become Jews, Christians all too easily came to repudiate those who repudiated them. Thus Jews became a convenient source of any and all troubles in Christendom. The situation can be summed up in a familiar bit of doggerel:

How odd of God to choose the Jews ...

with its reply:

But not so odd as those who choose
A Jewish God, but spurn the Jews.

On the Friday that Christians call Good, the day on which they commemorate the crucifixion of Jesus, it was one of the nastier customs of medieval Christendom to find Jews to whom some mischief could be done, which was argued in folk custom to be the enacting of revenge upon those who killed Jesus. "Christ killers," the Jews were called, and no form of harassment or humiliation was spared. Jews commonly hid in their ghettos on Good Friday lest they be attacked by marauding bands of Christians out to avenge the savior who, incidentally, happened to be Jewish himself.

Martin Luther was, alas, a virulent anti-Semite. In his translation of the Bible into German, he boasted, he had so transformed Moses and Jesus into Germans that no one would know they were Jewish. The church that bears Luther's name would eventually, in modern times, apologize for his hateful xenophobia; and the Roman Catholic church, whose reformation was Luther's chief objective, would absolve the Jews of responsibility for the death of Jesus and, in the heroic pilgrimages of John Paul II, make public apology for Roman Catholic anti-Semitism.

The Roman church realized it had the wrong end of the moral stick in the matter of the Jews and Jesus, and the Jews and the church, and it was painful to remember what it had done and in what it had been complicit. On Good Friday, Christians used to be expected to pray for the conversion of the Jews, but nowadays, among other things for which prayers are offered on Good Friday, Christians pray to be forgiven for harm done to the Jews in the name of the church.

In the General Confession in the Book of Common Prayer, having bewailed "our manifold sins and wickedness, which we from time to time most grievously have committed by thought, word, and deed …," the people are required to acknowledge a psychological reality:

The remembrance of them is grievous unto us; the burden of them is intolerable.

The remembrance of things past, especially of things we have managed to get wrong in the past, is painful, but also very necessary.

Reformation Day

Among the most vivid memories I have of my pre-ecumenical youth in a small, largely Protestant town is the annual celebration of Reformation Day on the Sunday nearest to Halloween. All the Protestant churchgoers would gather in one of the larger churches on that Sunday afternoon, ostensibly to celebrate the nailing of Luther's theses to the church door in Wittenberg, which in 1517 started the Reformation, but actually to celebrate the fact that we were not Catholics. Catholics were largely of immigrant stock and kept to the religion of the old country, doing everything the pope, through their priests, told them to do. Catholics, we all knew, didn't think for themselves, refrained from eating meat on Fridays, were conspicuous with their ashes on Ash Wednesday, had their throats blessed on Saint Blaise's Day, and generally voted Democratic. They were not to be trusted. Our friends who went to parochial schools were lost to society, and the mere thought of a Roman Catholic president of the United States made many people very nervous.

On Reformation Day we sang Luther's great hymn, "A Mighty Fortress Is Our God," with more gusto than usual, and we reminded ourselves of such Catholic misadventures as the Crusades, the Spanish Inquisition, and the pope's refusal to take seriously the scientific work of Galileo. Although we were too polite to speak of such things in public, especially in church, many referred in private to the Vatican as the "Whore of Babylon," to use a term dear to the Puritans and found in the book of Revelation. The Knights of Columbus was a sinister organization of Masonic wannabes, and we all knew about those infamous tunnels that connected convents to rectories. Nuns were bald and dangerous, and priests told the faithful never to enter a Protestant church and to make the sign of the cross whenever they passed one. Marriage to a Protestant placed the Catholic outside the church, and any issue of the marriage was assumed to be illegitimate. On this last point I was particularly sensitive, as my father was a lapsed Catholic and my mother an arch-Protestant. When some nuns attempted to reclaim my father for the church of his Portuguese ancestors, they told him that he should regard his wife, my mother, as his sister. "What about the boy?" my father asked, and was not happy with the answer. He never went back.

These were the things we Protestants "knew" to be true, and while we lived, worked, and even had social contact with Catholics, we simply knew that they were alien, wrong, and, in too large an aggregate, dangerous. As if to solidify our prejudices we gathered on Reformation Day to celebrate our differences, by which we meant our superiority. On one of those occasions the churches combined to bring as a guest speaker a man, Emmett McLoughlin, who had gained considerable notoriety as a former priest. His book exposing the Roman Catholic church was almost as popular as the equally famous anticommunist book *I Led Three Lives* by the counterspy Herbert A. Philbrick.

Anti-Catholicism was a low-grade fever among us, with few free from its infection. John F. Kennedy, our junior senator from Massachusetts, would have to tell the Southern Baptists and, by proxy, the rest of us Protestants, that being a Roman Catholic would have nothing whatsoever to do with the discharge of his public duties as president. Even with that, he defeated Richard Nixon by the narrowest of margins—winning only because, some die-hard Protestants would argue, of the remarkable capacity of the dead to vote in Chicago.

It would take a Catholic to remove the stain of anti-Catholicism from polite society, and that Catholic was good Pope John XXIII, whose calling of the Second Vatican Council opened an era of new relations between Catholics and Protestants. Protestant observers were invited to attend the sessions of Vatican II, and even Harvard University, founded by anti-Catholic Puritans, created a chair in Roman Catholic Theological Studies in the Faculty of Divinity. There were some prominent members of that faculty, including George Buttrick and Paul Tillich, who questioned the wisdom of the move, but it was clear that the time had come to put away as much of the old animosity and ignorance as possible, and that this appointment was one way to do it.

By the mid-1960s, Reformation Day as a celebration of anti-Catholicism was a thing of the past, as Protestants studied Roman Catholic theology and Catholics began to sing Protestant hymns. Fifty years ago, one would not have imagined a Supreme Court with a majority of Roman Catholic justices, much less successful political alliances between conservative Roman Catholics and evangelical Protestants; and who would ever have imagined that Billy Graham and Pope John Paul II would be on the same list of highly regarded moral leaders of the twentieth century? In England a Roman Catholic may not stand in succession to the throne, nor may anyone in the succession marry a Roman Catholic without forfeiting his or her position in the succession; the former Prime Minister, however, is married to a Roman Catholic and their children are being reared as such. The very least of United States presidential candidate John F. Kerry's problems was the fact that he was a practicing Roman Catholic. How is it that for so long, so many could get so much so wrong?

Woman's Place

Today it is almost impossible to watch the host of programs broadcast by televangelists without seeing women in prominent places preaching, teaching, exhorting, writing books—doing all the things once reserved for male evangelists and preachers. All of this happens in churches with what is called a "high doctrine of scripture," where presumably the literal reading of scripture, which is characteristically the red meat of those traditions, is understood differently with regard to the Pauline prohibitions against female preaching and teaching. Even the black denominations, which are traditionally more conservative than their white equivalents, have transformed many of their prejudices about women in the pulpit. The African Methodist Episcopal church has at least one female bishop, and our local AME church in Plymouth, Massachusetts, has had at least three female ministers in recent years.

My mother was a preacher's daughter and eventually a preacher's mother, yet I remember her early aversion to women in leadership roles in our local Baptist church. We had a woman in our church who was a talented Bible teacher, possessed of a certain charisma and with a great gift for words, who would from time to time "supply the pulpit," as we used to say, much to the dismay of my mother and a few others. When I asked what was wrong with Mrs. Wilson's preaching, my mother replied that it was "unseemly" and "contrary to scripture." That, however, was occasional; she really got onto her theological high horse when our church decided to elect female deacons and to encourage more female preachers. We had always had deaconesses, who were by definition the wives of the deacons. The office of deacon dated from New Testament times, and deacons were second only to the pastor in the exercise of spiritual authority in the church. The deaconesses' role, by contrast, was to prepare the Lord's table, wash the linens and the little glasses in which the grape juice was served, and otherwise make themselves useful by acts of charity and kindness. Nevertheless, a woman deacon was a quite regular, visible, permanent part of the local ecclesiastical establishment. A woman preacher, however, although not officially forbidden, was a rare and curious thing, "like a dog walking on its hind legs," as Samuel Johnson once observed. From such an innovation as women preachers there would be no turning back, and, as my mother and others would say, it would attract the wrong kind of woman, for who could take spiritual authority from such a person?

We have had female deacons for quite a long time now, and the sky has not fallen. In the summer of 2006, the Episcopalians elected a female presiding bishop, which made news, but not as much as the fact that earlier in that year the Episcopalians in California did not elect a homosexual as their diocesan bishop. There are female rabbis, and there are female clergy in nearly every Christian denomination; only Southern Baptists and Roman Catholics withhold ordination from women, and with those two groups scripture and tradition serve to sustain their cultural prejudices. Everywhere else in the West, however, the old ecclesiastical inhibitions concerning women are seen not simply as old-fashioned—"unseemly," as my mother's generation would say—but as wrong. The same Bible that was once read to keep women out is now understood to call for their full inclusion in the life of the church and, most particularly, in its leadership. An inclusive church requires no less than this, and once again we might ask how so many for so long could be so wrong about so much.

Who's In? Who's Out?

There is a hoary joke among the clergy that describes a guided tour of heaven. The guide takes the visitor through a splendid palace, each room filled with a group of merrymakers. The visitor sees the Baptists in one room dancing, which was forbidden on earth; the Methodists in another room drinking; the Presbyterians in a large space enjoying unaccustomed chaos; and the Roman Catholics in another large space enjoying guilt without sex. As they turn a corner and approach yet another large room, the guide says, "We must be quiet now; these are the Episcopalians, and they think they're the only ones here." The reader is free to substitute the denomination of his or her choice, but the point is there to be made. Some people cannot imagine anyone else in their eternity; they imagine heaven to be as exclusive as their own church, filled with remarkably similar people.

Can serious Christians seriously believe that they are the only ones upon whom God has placed his blessings? If we take the Bible seriously, how do we explain that the notion of a chosen people is one that expands rather than contracts? If Jesus Christ is the center of the biblical witness and the one in whom all that we know about God is to be found, how do we reconcile his expansive and inclusive behavior as recorded in scripture with what has so often been the constricted and exclusive practice of the church?

Some of us are old enough to remember the chorus once popular among evangelical youth:

Turn your eyes upon Jesus,
Look full in his wonderful face,

And the things of earth will grow strangely dim,
In the light of his glory and grace.[1]

We have many times rehearsed the fact that Jesus embraced as his own those who were excluded by the respectably religious of his day, and that he was not only a friend to sinners but a friend of those whom the righteous chose to avoid. Jesus' generosity and hospitality got him into terrible trouble with those who believed it was their job to maintain the standards of probity and the law; we should all shudder at the prospect of having to face him, with the duty of giving an account of how we treated those with whom he would have been so generous. Nowhere in scripture do we find the mantra "Love the sinner and hate the sin"; history has shown that it is the "sinner" rather than the sin that is usually ostracized, criticized, and even crucified. The "least of these" are least not by Jesus' standards but by the standards of the world, and we deceive only ourselves when we say that we are maintaining the purity of the church and its ministry in Jesus' name and for his sake.

Many years ago, I was preparing to preach as a guest minister in a very posh church, and just as the rector and I were about to proceed to our prayers before the service, a wildly disoriented young man burst into the room. He spoke loudly but nonsensically, seemingly either "on" or "off" something. Whatever it was, though, his erratic behavior was familiar to the rector, who treated him with enormous but firm courtesy and let the little tantrum run its course. The intruder left as abruptly as he had arrived, and while I was shaken the rector was not, and was clearly used to such interruptions. As we pulled ourselves back together, his thoughtful comment was, "I keep hoping it isn't Jesus."

Jesus was no demoniac—John the Baptist was probably more terrifying—but when I think of Jesus, I think not of a polite and socially acceptable young Christian or of a professional theologian or devout parishioner; I think of the people with whom Jesus associated, of how he confused his friends the disciples and terrified even his most powerful enemies, including King Herod, who worried about the rumor of a mere baby as a rival. I think of the man who invited himself to Zacchaeus's house for lunch and bandied words with a Samaritan woman at a well. I think of the man who rebuked his own careful followers when they condemned the erotic impertinence of the woman who washed his feet with her hair. I think of the man whose silent dignity intimidated Pontius Pilate in his own judgment hall. This Jesus, I fear, would have had very little patience with the likes of us, who push people around, ignore his commandment to love, and use his name for our own devices. I often wonder if those who expect Jesus to return any day now are really prepared to meet him, and to answer his question about what we did with, for, and to the "least."

It will not be hard for many to demonstrate that they have obeyed the rules, and many will be able to cite significant gestures of Christian charity. Possibly there will be some among them who have practiced tithing; check stubs, it is said, tell a great deal about one's sense of social responsibility. I am certain too that there will be many who will be able to give an account of how well they lived their private lives, how kindly they treated their families, and how generous they were in the church with their time, talent, and treasure. I cannot believe, however, that Jesus will be impressed with any of this. He was not impressed the first time around, and what has there been in the intervening millennia to suggest that his standards have changed? One longs for the day of the Lord with a certain fear and trembling, for in the final judgment we will be held to account not on the basis of what we know or of what we believe. Jesus, I suspect, has little interest in doctrinal sophistication. We will be held accountable for what we did, and how we reconciled what we did or did not do with what we knew to be the righteous intentions that we should show toward the least.

We continue to make amends for our treatment of God's people, the Jews. We are working on our relationships with previously excluded women and the sins of racism, and some are taking stewardship of the earth more seriously while, slowly, many are waking up to the realities of God's wider creation of "others," even if they happen to be non-Christians.

If there remains one area in which our parochial obduracy continues to obtain, however, it is in the church's treatment of its homosexual brothers and sisters; if there is an area in which we are to be weighed and found wanting, this is it. It is not out of ignorance alone that we behave as we do toward sexual minorities; it is out of ignorance, fear, and, in certain cases, malice. None of it is excusable: private judgment on sexual matters does not excuse our unwillingness to include in full participation in the household of faith those who engage in sex differently. Two generations of biblical scholarship have shown that the scriptures cannot be used as a basis for our discrimination on the subject of homosexuality, so why are our churches as divided on this subject today as they were a generation ago on the subject of women, or a century ago on the subject of slavery?

More than a decade ago I wrote a book on how to read the Bible in which I argued that it is to be read with mind and heart and in the light of the mind of Christ, with the assistance of nearly two thousand years of accumulated wisdom. The Bible, I argued, is a library, not a textbook, and there are some things in it that are rooted in the practices of the time in which its books were written. The treatment of women, the assumptions about chattel slavery, even certain views of God, such as "The Lord is a man of war," should be located within the timeframe of human authors. More important are those biblical principles that extend beyond the limits of social location and are always and everywhere true: the love of God and neighbor, the example of Jesus Christ, the call to discipleship and service, God's mercy and justice, and, as Roman Catholic theology puts it, the preferential option for the poor. We as believers were never meant to be frozen into a historically biblical point of view, but to go and grow toward that to which the Bible points: the gospel, the good news. Jesus, after all, did not come to teach the Bible; he came, as the Bible says more than once, to preach the good news.

Thus I have been disappointed, to say the least, to find that the Bible becomes the first refuge of those who are unwilling to reconsider their extrabiblical prejudices against including homosexuals in the full life and ministry of the church. I had hoped that, as has happened with women and racial minorities, our predominantly Christian culture would recognize that God's children, the homosexuals in our midst, cry out for our compassion and acceptance. In this decade, alas, exactly the opposite has happened. Positions have hardened and homosexuals have been demonized, condemned to a "lifestyle" rather than invited to a life in the household of faith. It amazes me that any thoughtful homosexuals would continue to want any part of a community, religious or otherwise, that in the name of God has behaved toward them with such contempt.

Arguments and reasoned debate seem beside the point. Those religionists who are not exhausted by the debate seem inclined to draw a line in the sand, by which homosexuality is deemed beyond the pale of Christian acceptance. Even the war on terror does not heat up the churches to the same degree as the seemingly endless debates about homosexuality and what the church should or should not do about those homosexuals who wish to participate in the church on an equal basis with everyone else; it almost seems as though we need someone to despise in order to feel good about ourselves. Divorce continues to do great damage to the ideal of the Christian family, and Jesus' views on divorce are unambiguous: he is against it. Yet the Episcopalians, the United Methodists, and the

Presbyterians, to mention only three of the largest Protestant denominations, find their councils locked in mortal combat on the subject of homosexuality. Even abortion comes in second to the passions that homosexuality seems to arouse in otherwise quite sensible people.

How can we conduct a debate on the subject of homosexuality when the Bible is silent on the subject in terms that are most relevant to our own times? When *The Good Book: Reading the Bible with Mind and Heart* was published, I was criticized by some for being hard on people whose views on homosexuality do not square with my own, while others felt that I was too irenic toward those who make homosexuality the last acceptable prejudice and the Bible the chief weapon in affirming that prejudice. People outside the Christian community wonder what all the fuss is about, many within the Christian community are discouraged by militant homophobia, and too many in the Christian community see homosexuality as the only available proxy to be fought in the pervasive culture wars. With so much going wrong in the world, one might think that we would have more important things with which to concern ourselves.

For Freedom Christ Has Set Us Free?

From what has Christ set us free? That is the question to which Paul gives the answer in his furious letter to the Galatians, and that letter just might prove helpful as we consider who is in and who is out in the large claims of the gospel. For these insights I am grateful to H. Darrell Lance, Professor of New Testament at Colgate Rochester Crozer Divinity School, who for a decade has edited *The InSpiriter*, the newsletter of the Association of Welcoming & Affirming Baptists. In the summer 2006 issue, Professor Lance offers an instructive commentary on Paul's letter to the Galatians, in which the debate was over circumcision. Paul found it unnecessary for Gentiles to be circumcised—he was, after all, the apostle to the Gentiles. Jewish Christians, however, thought otherwise. While Paul was in Galatia his teachings prevailed, but when he went away the influence of the Jewish Christian teachers began to take hold. Paul is furious when he learns that his teaching is being undermined by a group of articulate, convincing, but, in his opinion, wrong-headed spiritual leaders. For Paul, joy came with salvation in Christ, not through a blind obedience to the law, and thus he begins with the famous salutation: "You foolish Galatians! Who has bewitched you?" An even more emphatic rendering is found in the Revised English Bible:

> O foolish Galatians! Who has bewitched you, before whose eyes Jesus Christ was publicly portrayed as crucified? Let me ask you only this: did you receive the Spirit by works of the law, or by hearing with faith? Are you so foolish?[2]

Professor Lance paraphrases the verses addressed to the "poor confused Galatians":

> Are we to believe Paul and our own experience, or these other teachers who seem so sincere and confident in their teaching? These teachers say they are only telling us what is for our own good. They are concerned for our salvation. They say it is because they love us that they are teaching us the truth, that we must be circumcised to be truly Christian. What are we to do?[3]

The answer, says Paul:

> In Christ Jesus neither circumcision nor uncircumcision counts for anything; the only thing that counts is faith working through love.[4]

"Faith working through love" is all that matters, not religious purity, not circumcision, and, Lance adds, "Not even—dare we say it?—heterosexuality." Then Lance suggests that if in reading Galatians we substitute "heterosexuality" for "circumcision," we have an almost exact parallel. The traditionalist position on the gay issue would be to say, in Lance's words again,

> that the Pharisees of Jesus' day and the "Circumcision Party" of Paul's day were right after all. . . .
>
> It would be to deny that we are saved by grace through faith. So nothing less than the nature of the Gospel itself is at stake in the battle over homosexuality.

This is a bold claim that can easily be written off as a partisan, pro-homosexuality view, but to do so would be a serious and dangerous mistake. It is not a matter of inserting homosexuality where it doesn't belong; it is a question of refusing to allow the gospel to expand beyond the boundaries of our own limited comfort zone. Surely, the "Circumcision Party" in Galatia felt that it was doing the right thing for the right reason, and in their rectitude its members failed to see that the only standard for Christian inclusivity is faith working through love: it was for this that Christ came and died on the cross, and it will be by this standard alone that we all will be judged. That is the gospel, and that is why we call it the good news. It points beyond the pages of the Bible, and even beyond the history in which it is found, to an inclusive, comprehensive future in which all of God's creation is to be embraced.

What Is the Spirit Saying to the Churches?

In the years of this overheated debate on homosexuality and the churches, I have found it, while difficult, easier to persuade my homosexual brothers and sisters that God loves them than that many of their heterosexual brothers and sisters love them. The Bible has been used as a blunt instrument to exclude those whose differences make us uncomfortable by those who claim to be maintaining "biblical standards." Such application of the scriptures to support the cultural status quo privileges the conventional wisdom, making the Bible a tool of oppression, the church an exclusive fellowship of shared prejudice, and the glad tidings—the gospel that Jesus came to proclaim—a mockery.

This is not the first time that change has been challenged by a powerful conformity. The means that allows the winds of change to blow through the corridors of conformity is the powerful work of the Spirit, that third member of the Trinity that makes the church a slave neither to history nor to the moment, but rather an agency of transformation. The key to God's will for the church is not found in text or in history, but rather by reverent and radical listening to what the Spirit has to say to the churches, an attitude grounded neither in civil law nor in social science. If the Spirit were not alive and speaking to the churches, and if believers had never listened and responded to what the Spirit had to say, Christianity would still be a Jewish sect struggling with the law, women would remain silent and subordinated, and slavery would still be the order of the day for those powerful enough to compel others to submit to them. Scripture without the Spirit would be a dead letter, and the church without the Spirit would be a museum.

Jeffrey S. Siker, Professor and Chair of the Department of Theological Studies and a scholar of New Testament at Loyola Marymount University in Los Angeles, argues that Paul, believing himself led by the Spirit, "believed [on that authority] that the experiences of Gentile Christians confirmed their reception of the Spirit apart from the law."[5] He suggests that the author of Acts makes the same point in Acts 10, with reference to the Gentile Cornelius. Cornelius does not have to become a law-observant Jew in order to have proper faith in Christ; God was doing a new thing, Siker argues:

> Paul and Peter were calling on the church to acknowledge what God was doing, even though it scandalized the church and seemed to go against scripture tradition.[6]

Scripture calls us to pay attention to the Spirit and to follow its lead. We do not read scripture in the twenty-first century in the same way that people read it in the sixteenth, nineteenth, twentieth, or any other century. It is through the Spirit that we approach the gospel beyond the limits of text and time, and that is why the church must always be a listening community, for when it fails to listen, it runs the risk of substituting its own convictions for what God intends through the Spirit. We must not only listen to the Spirit, we must listen to the witness of the faithful, many of whom may be homosexual, whose testimony is suppressed at the risk of the church's own integrity. Siker writes:

> Scripture calls upon us in the church today to pay attention to the testimony of God's Spirit as we have experienced the profound faith of gay and lesbian Christians in our midst. As Peter told the Jerusalem assembly, "If God gave [Cornelius's household] the same gift that he gave us when we believed in the Lord Jesus Christ, who was I that I could hinder God?" (Acts 11:17) Surely we must see them first of all as brothers and sisters who do not cease to be gay or lesbian by virtue of their Christian faith.[7]

A Challenge from the Grave

For many, the late William Sloane Coffin, Yale chaplain, minister of Riverside Church, and social gadfly, who died in April 2006, much mourned and missed, was a profound irritant. He had an enormous capacity for annoying even his friends, and there are still many who think of him as just one more loud voice on the loony left, but if ever there was a man who embodied the image of the prophet as one who "afflicted the comfortable and comforted the afflicted," it was Bill Coffin. Those who disliked him usually did so because he violated their comfort zone with the unappealing claims of the gospel. In a 1999 talk at Harvard Divinity School, he put the matter of his Christian faith on the line for all would-be believers, leaders, and followers:

> Let Christians remember how Jesus was concerned most for those society counted least and put last. Let us all remember what Martin Luther King Jr. and Gandhi never forgot—how frequently compassion demands confrontation.[8]

He reminded his listeners, many of whom were preparing for conventional service in conventional churches, that

> Jesus subverted the conventional religious wisdom of his time. We have to do the same. The answer to bad evangelism is not no evangelism but good evangelism. Good evangelism is not proselytizing but witnessing, bearing witness to "the light that shines in the darkness, and the darkness has not overcome it"; bearing witness to the prophet's cry: "Let justice roll down like mighty waters," and to the prophetic insight that we all belong one to another, every one from the pope to the loneliest wino on the planet.[9]

The title of his talk was "The Politics of Compassion: The Heart Is a Little to the Left." His are words worth heeding even as they come to us from beyond the grave. If the gospel is truly good news, it has to be good news for everyone, for it is either an inclusive gospel or no gospel at all. Prejudice, paranoia, the politics of exclusion—all these little systems have their day, and there are moments when they appear to prevail, but the church, we know from experience, will eventually do the right thing once it has exhausted every other alternative. We who struggle today know that a social gospel and an inclusive gospel are the consequences of a hopeful gospel. In a world surrounded on every hand by bad news, we turn now to the reasonable hope of the gospel, the good news toward which scripture, Jesus, and the Spirit all point.

A Gospel of Hope

For if you find hope in the ground of history, you are united with the great prophets who were able to look into the depth of their times, who tried to escape it, because they could not stand the horror of their visions, and who yet had the strength to look to an even deeper level and there to discover hope.

—Paul Tillich,
*The Shaking of
the Foundations*

May the God of hope fill you with all joy and peace in believing, so that you may abound in hope by the power of the Holy Spirit.

—Romans 15:13

I am a man of hope, not for human reasons nor from any natural optimism, but because I believe the Holy Spirit is at work in the Church and in the world, even when His name remains unheard.

—Léon Joseph
Cardinal Suenens

I keep turning over in my mind the occasion, now more than twenty years ago, on which I welcomed the South African novelist Alan Paton to The Memorial Church. He was perhaps the most famous South African before Nelson Mandela, his fame deriving in large part from *Cry, the Beloved Country*, his novel about life in apartheid-ridden South Africa, which had by then achieved the status of a classic. Paton, a white man, was unusual in writing with sympathy, even passion, about the tragic consequences of his country's racism, and many thought of him as a countercultural force for good in a land that at the time seemed immune to external pressures for reform. Events, however, were overtaking Paton, who as an older man watched a new generation of black leaders such as Steve Biko and Desmond Tutu take their places at the front of what would become a worldwide movement against apartheid. By the time of his Harvard visit Paton seemed rather old-fashioned, and his novel, famous to an earlier generation, dated.

He gave three lectures, more autobiographical reflections and scriptural commentary than sustained analysis, and yet his moral presence was significant and he drew large, divided crowds. A lot of older people came to hear him out of admiration, and a lot of black South African exiles came out of anger that still their country should be represented in the West by an old white novelist. At the end of the third lecture, the questions came fast and furious, and I will always remember one exchange. A "Cambridge lady," one of those whom the poet e. e. cummings once described as living in "furnished souls," rose to her feet and asked, "Given all that you have said and we have heard, are you optimistic about the future for your beloved country?" Paton paused, scowled, and said, "Madam, I am not optimistic, but I remain hopeful." He did not expand upon his distinction between optimism and hope, but I have thought about it ever since. I too think there is a useful, even helpful, distinction to be made.

The cynic Ambrose Bierce, in his *Devil's Dictionary*, defines optimism as:

The doctrine, or belief that everything is beautiful, including what is ugly, everything good, especially the bad, and everything right that is wrong ... an intellectual disorder, yielding to no treatment but death.

Voltaire, writing in 1739 in *Candide*, spoke of optimism as

... the madness of maintaining that everything is right when it is wrong.

The Methodist preacher Halford E. Luccock, writing in 1957 during America's season of cheery, religious expansion as represented by such figures as Norman Vincent Peale and Dale Carnegie, observed rather tartly that

Christianity did not come into the world with a fixed, silly grin on its face and a vapid "Cheerio!" on its lips. At its center was a cross. That heritage must be saved from being perverted by the bright-side boys, whether in the pulpit or out of it.[1]

The age of optimism had as its unofficial motto the madly popular psycho-mantra of Monsieur Coué, who in the 1920s had nearly everyone convinced that "Every day in every way I am getting better and better." America in the first half of the twentieth century was well supplied with "Optimist" clubs, which regarded the power of positive thinking as essential to the American creed. Moreover, the constitutionally guaranteed right to the pursuit of happiness was fueled by optimism. Optimism and opportunity went hand in hand: no one made the pioneer wagon journey across the American continent expecting to fail, most people expected that they would end better than they had begun, and to "accentuate the positive" was almost the moral imperative of citizenship. Optimism was as American as apple pie.

One of the earliest criticisms of what would later be called the civil rights movement was that it emphasized what was wrong with America rather than what was right. The issue of race was divisive, not only in the south, which had never yet come to terms with the loss of the Civil War, but also in the rest of the country, where the illusion of civil harmony was essential to the sense of order. It was considered bad form when in the 1920s and 1930s from the Manhattan headquarters of the NAACP a banner was hung for all to see: A COLORED MAN WAS LYNCHED TODAY. When President Hoover, on the heels of "Coolidge prosperity" and at the dawn of the Great Depression, uttered his famous "Prosperity is just around the corner," Americans not only wished it to be so but believed that it was.

In general, the American habit of religious revival stemmed from the conviction that a second and better chance at goodness was always available. Three American-based religious movements in particular were grounded in this culture of optimism. Mary Baker Eddy's remarkably successful Christian Science movement developed out of her optimism that mind was superior to matter, and that by the spiritual disciplines of the mind, healing could be accomplished in ways not seen since the biblical age of miracles. The Church of Jesus Christ of Latter Day Saints, whose members are more familiarly known as Mormons, believed that its new revelation of an ancient religion could be realized ultimately by gathering the saints in a new promised land in the vicinity of the valley of the Great Salt Lake. Mr. Rutherford's Jehovah's Witnesses believed that God's ultimate righteous justice would be made real in a twentieth-century Armageddon, and that if we read The Watchtower and believed what the intrepid door-to-door evangelists had to say, we could join the saved and inherit both heaven and a purged earth.

The spirit of American religious optimism was deeply ingrained in the American psyche, and not limited to those three American-born religious communities. The gospel of prosperity is alive and well in contemporary America, as a casual glance at televangelism will reveal. The shelves of religious bookstores groan with volumes on self-improvement and prosperity and with tales of religious derring-do, all grounded in the creed of optimism.

So what is wrong with optimism? The worst that can be said about optimism is that, if we are not careful, it seduces us into looking at the bright side at the risk of failing to take reality seriously. The saddest figure of the twentieth century was Prime Minister Neville Chamberlain of Great Britain, who, having seen what World War I had done to an entire generation, with all his heart hoped to avert another terrible European war. He would do whatever it took to avoid a new iteration of that conflict, and so he went to Munich to try to persuade Adolf Hitler not to proceed with his expansionist plans at the expense of the small countries of Europe. In a famous photograph taken at the airfield on his return to England, the Prime Minister is shown waving a piece of paper, presumably a memorandum of understanding between himself and Hitler, while declaring "peace in our time."

Winston Churchill, then in opposition, was roundly derided for his pessimistic views on German rearmament. He was in his so-called wilderness years because he recognized, as did few others, that Hitler was an unreconstructed menace and could not be trusted, no matter what he signed or said. Moreover, he knew that neither Britain nor France was prepared at that moment to resist an aggressive Germany. In the movie *The Remains of the Day*, we see with what mindless optimism members of the British establishment looked at the world situation, and how that optimism obscured their grasp on reality. Chamberlain so much wanted peace, and so believed that it was obtainable between gentlemen, that he could not, would not, see the dangerous reality at hand. In hindsight we recognize how naïve, no, how plain wrong he was, and when war came and had to be fought, it was Churchill who was sent for.

The Ambiguity of Hope

One of my least favorite liturgical seasons is Advent, which comprises the four weeks that follow Thanksgiving and precede Christmas. The conventional wisdom is that Advent is the season of hope, and we light our Advent candles, one more on each Sunday, not simply anticipating the light but increasing it. Although Advent is, like Lent, meant to be a season of penitence, hope as a theme has long triumphed over the mood of repentance, and I do not criticize Advent because, to all intents and purposes, it has become a month-long dress rehearsal for Christmas and a commercial phenomenon that is beyond the power of mere Christians to defeat. Years ago, when in October I saw the first Santa Claus in a store window and heard tinny carols in a department store elevator, I knew that Thanksgiving could not be far away and that the battle for Advent had been lost. What I find difficult to take seriously about Advent is the note of false rather than authentic hope that is imposed upon people.

I watch congregations struggle with the Advent hymns. In my own congregation, we begin every Advent Sunday with the popular hymn "O Come, O Come, Emmanuel," the final verse of which tells us what to expect:

O come, Desire of nations, bind
All peoples in one heart and mind;

Bid envy, strife, and quarrels cease;
Fill the whole world with heaven's peace.

The irony is that envy, strife, and quarreling are very much the order of the day; the world is hardly filled with heaven's peace. Are we praying for the restoration of some imagined time of bliss and satisfaction, or, despite the evidence of our own experience, are we looking toward something that has not yet been achieved? Preachers struggle mightily to preach sermons that make sense of the Advent hope, and that is not easy to do. The facts inevitably make us work hard around the concept of hope, and not too many Advents ago I concluded that I know more of humbug than of hope, and this I would share with a congregation for whom the Advent hope had become something of a cliché. Humbug I know. Humbug I see. The world is full of humbug, and it does not take a great imagination to realize that.

How many times have I watched televised versions of Dickens's *A Christmas Carol*, in which my favorite character, Ebenezer Scrooge, utters his famous epithet, "Bah! Humbug!" He does so, you'll recall, when well-meaning solicitors call at his office for a contribution for the relief of the poor. Here he asks his infamous question about workhouses, orphanages, and the other institutions to which the poor are meant to resort, but he has heard before all that the do-gooders have to say and he sees that their good works remain ineffective. The solicitors think he wishes to remain anonymous in charity, but he simply wishes to be left alone, and he sends them off with nothing. Scrooge will not submit to emotional extortion.

Some of us know how he feels, for the season is rife with emotional extortion, and while we are meant to subsidize "tidings of comfort and joy," there seems to be very little comfort and joy about us. In some instances the iconic office Christmas party is filled with anything but comfort and joy, and sometimes the introduction of "secret Santa" and staff raffles makes us irritable and irritating.

The secular culture that has no theology to speak of, much less a Christian one, tends to define this season in terms of charity and optimism, and we are all meant to play our parts or feel guilty for not doing so, yet the world in December almost always seems as precarious as ever. The season does not afford our leaders any more wisdom than usual, and although we look for quick fixes, there are none to be had. It may be an urban legend, but psychologists and psychiatrists tell us that this is the season of the most intense mental distress and depression. Why should that be? In part, I think, because people prefer hope to humbug, and are invariably disappointed when humbug prevails and experience triumphs over hope. This year, we tell ourselves—and the conventional wisdom encourages us to hope for such things—Christmas will see the wonderful reunion of families and our dreadful relatives will be less dreadful, but the facts tell another story.

Surely, however, it ought to be better in the church than in the secular world of manufactured good cheer? Surely our hope is not misplaced? Surely we are not investing in a naïve image of a world that never was and never can be? Surely there is a dose of realistic hope? I wonder: I genuinely, truly wonder.

Many years ago, I assisted as an extra pair of clerical hands at the Christmas Eve service in Boston's historic and splendid Trinity Church. The crowd waiting to get into the church from Copley Square, on which the church fronts, was so great and so agitated that a detachment of mounted police had to be dispatched for crowd control. The scene outside the church looked like the prelude to a rock concert, and inside there were wall-to-wall people, not the usual Sunday worshipers but a rather odd collection of people waiting for something to happen. They sang the familiar carols with gusto, but the rest of the liturgy seemed unfamiliar to most of them. Then, in their hundreds, they accepted the invitation to come to the communion rail. The church was beautifully decorated, the music incredibly grand, and the general effect pregnant with expectation. At the rail, after I had given the cup to one young man, through his tears he asked, "Now what happens, now what do I do?" I told him to go back to his seat as there were people waiting for his place at the rail. It was an inadequate response; perhaps I might have given him Emily Dickinson's lines about hope:

> *Hope is the thing with feathers*
> *That perches in the soul*
> *And sings the tune without the words*
> *And never stops at all.*[2]

Rather than the hope of organized good cheer, Dickinson's image offers an elusive, fleeting clarity, vividly vague, as it were, that endures in the most intimate of spaces and never gives up. Hope, in her view, is not a policy or a doctrine or a form of nostalgia either theological or secular. It is, rather, "the thing with feathers that perches in the soul." I like the use of the word "perches" here, with its suggestion of the precarious or delicately balanced. There is something fragile about it and yet it abides, however precariously, at the very center of our being—the "thing with feathers." Perhaps it was such a precarious hope that had brought the young man to the altar that night: I wished I had better served him.

When the poet Henry Wadsworth Longfellow wrote his once very popular hymn "I Heard the Bells on Christmas Day," he spoke to the ambiguity of hope, a hope that seemed precarious, even mocking, at the time of the American Civil War. The first verse tells of what is expected:

I heard the bells on Christmas Day
Their old, familiar carols play,
And wild and sweet
The words repeat
Of peace on earth, good will to men!

Then reality sets in, and the contrast between what the bells say and the actual state of the world is painfully obvious:

Then from each black, accursed mouth
The cannon thundered in the South,
And with the sound
The carols drowned
Of peace on earth, good will to men!

And in despair I bowed my head;
"There is no peace on earth," I said;
"For hate is strong,
And mocks the song
Of peace on earth, good will to men."

Good Victorian that he was, however, Longfellow concludes with an affirmation of hope that stands the test of time:

Then pealed the bells more loud and deep;
"God is not dead, nor doth He sleep;
The Wrong shall fail,
The Right prevail,
With peace on earth, good will to men."

When Phillips Brooks wrote his beloved carol "O Little Town of Bethlehem," he found himself facing the birth of the Christ child in a world where children's lives were devalued by violence and poverty, and the current world as disagreeable a place as ever it was, the progress and prosperity of the nineteenth century notwithstanding. The original fourth verse, the "grim" verse, as it is often called, of his carol is usually omitted from modern hymnbooks, and thus Brooks seems to be writing of a nostalgic age now long gone, but its inclusion suggests that the hope of the Holy Child is not just sentiment but is grounded in the reality of Brooks's world, and, alas, our own:

> *Where children pure and happy pray to the blessed Child,*
> *Where misery cries out to Thee, Son of the mother mild;*
> *Where charity stands watching and faith holds wide the door,*
> *The dark night wakes, the glory breaks, and Christmas comes*
> *once more.*

Muscular Hope

We usually do not think of Saint Paul as a sentimental man, and it would be a wild stretch of the imagination to mention him in the same breath as the Belle of Amherst and her version of hope as "the thing with feathers," but could her hope be that hope of which Paul speaks in Romans 5? He writes:

Therefore, since we are justified by faith, we have peace with God through our Lord Jesus Christ, through whom we have obtained access to this grace in which we stand; and we boast in our hope of sharing the glory of God. And not only that, but we also boast in our sufferings, knowing that suffering produces endurance, and endurance produces character, and character produces hope, and hope does not disappoint us, because God's love has been poured into our hearts through the Holy Spirit that has been given to us.[3]

The Revised English Bible translates Romans 5:5 as: "Such hope is no fantasy."

Boasting in a hope that does not disappoint and is no fantasy is the kind of hope upon which we can depend, and that is the hope that Paul offers.

Dietrich Bonhoeffer once warned against cheap grace, and I warn now against cheap hope. Hope is not merely the optimistic view that somehow everything will turn out all right in the end if everyone just does as we do. Hope is the more rugged, the more muscular view that even if things don't turn out all right and aren't all right, we endure through and beyond the times that disappoint or threaten to destroy us. Something of the quality of that hope is found when the psalmist asks, "Why are you cast down, O my soul? Why are you disquieted within me? Hope in God, for I shall again praise him, my help and my God."

Muscular hope such as that of which Saint Paul speaks to the Romans comes with a price, and usually suffering and privation are involved. This kind of hope requires work, effort, and expenditure without the assurance of an easy or ready return. Paul's sequence reminds us of this: we pass from sufferings that are not avoided to endurance, which is the quality that allows us to keep on when it would be easier to quit. The process of enduring produces character, that inner quality not to be confused with image or reputation that is who we are when no one is looking. It is from character that hope is produced. This is where the old aphorism comes from that says, "Show me what you hope for, and I will know who you are."

Hope can seem a wimpy word, and it can be as flaccid as the typical Advent service, yet if we remember, as Paul reminds us, that genuine hope, a hope worth having, is forged upon the anvil of adversity, and that hope and suffering are related through the formation of character, then we will realize that hope is much more than mere optimism. Hope is the stuff that gets us through and beyond when the worst that can happen happens.

How Does Hope Work?

If we want to know how hope works, we must look first to those who suffer, for it is only in and through suffering that hope is made manifest. I do not endorse the cult of victimhood that often obsesses the African American community when it seeks to claim its place in the American scheme of things, but I do realize that the hope that has sustained African Americans through nearly four centuries of exploited experience in what is now the United States of America has been forged in the adversity of our people. This does not mean that adversity is good, or that all we have as a collectivity is a common adversity; it does mean that in the adversity forced upon us in many and various ways, we have been sustained by a hope that has seen us through.

On June 24, 2003, *The New York Times* carried an extensive review of the six-part PBS television series *This Far by Faith: African American Spiritual Journeys*, produced by Blackside, Inc., which also produced the memorable *Eyes on the Prize*, Henry Hampton's series. *This Far by Faith*, narrated by the black theologian James Cone, and other television documentaries of this type have become the device by which various aspects of our cultural past are made a part of our common experience. Although much is known of the role of religion in the shaping and preservation of the American black experience, this is by far the most authoritative and widely disseminated discussion of that topic. In the spirit of Ken Burns's iconic presentations on the Civil War and on baseball, *This Far by Faith* tells the story of religion and black America, with Sojourner Truth, Denmark Vesey, Henry McNeal Turner, and Thomas A. Dorsey emerging from Black History Month and African American Studies textbooks and entering into the nation's homes. The civil rights movement and contemporary issues, including the role of Islam in African American religion, compose the final installments in the series.

For anyone who takes religion and the African American experience seriously, the first and primary question will always be, How did a religion that was meant to make docile a captive people, the religion of their oppressors, become an instrument of liberation and transformation for the oppressed? Faith here is described as both a consolation and a catalyst. How could this be?

Part of the answer has to be found in the inherent truth of the faith, a truth that transcended the manipulations of those who used it for purposes of control. The African Americans' adoption of Christianity, an adoption often imposed, may well have been a strategy designed to confront those guilty of the moral evil of slavery on their own ground. It may well have been the path of least resistance, a conformity of necessity, as it were, but I think above all that the truth-claims of Jesus Christ were seen to be true despite their corruption at the hands of white Christians, and that those truths proved relevant to the condition of black men and women. If ever there was an experience of adversity in which a muscular hope could be forged, it was the experience of the African American in America, both in slavery and in freedom. The Christian church was the first social laboratory for the African American, and in the worst days of slavery, segregation, and the movement, Paul's sequence in Romans 5 was the pattern of the emerging community; no easy optimism would do here. Those people knew that "tribulation worketh patience; and patience, experience; and experience, hope: and hope maketh not ashamed ..."[4] This hope was no fantasy.

It has been said that while Christians are an optimistic people, Jews are a hopeful people. We find a perseverance of hope among the Jews throughout their long suffering, and for the Jews mere optimism will not do, for they have little about which to be optimistic. They are the people of the promises, the covenant, the people of Job and of the psalms, the people whose earthly homes have always been under assault but whose hope, even at Auschwitz, has never wavered. The kind of hope of which we speak, nourished by generations of suffering and frustration, is in the DNA of the Jewish people, who hope that people will behave better, particularly Christian people, but their ultimate hope is in God, who promised never to abandon them. With that hope, all suffering can be borne and overcome. The rabbis tell us that when a wise man was asked what he would do if he knew that the world was soon to end, the man replied that he would plant a tree. There is no more hopeful sign in the world than a tree planted in faith by one who will likely never see it in its maturity but whose experience, however limited, is sustained by hope grounded in God and nourished by suffering.

Hope works where nothing else does. If we want to know how and where hope works, we should look at the most desperate places and among people who suffer, for that is where hope is both necessary and evident. Hope, let us remember, is not the opposite of suffering; suffering is the necessary antecedent of hope.

Redeeming Revelation

In a remarkable study of the book of Revelation, New Testament scholar Barbara R. Rossing writes to counter the conventional wisdom that the last book of the Bible is a doomsday scenario of fear and terror fueled by the apocalyptic fantasies of Saint John the Divine:

Revelation is not a book written to inspire fear or terror. But it is definitely written to increase a sense of urgency for our world. It is an apocalyptic wake-up call for each of us, precisely because there is hope for us and for our world.[5]

What commands our attention here is the counterintuitive nature of Rossing's claim. Most people do not claim to know much about the book of Revelation, and most preachers tend to avoid it because of its vivid and complex imagery and the dangers associated with efforts to translate its dire predictions into applications relevant to the present-day life of believers. The exception to this reticence is found among those who see in Revelation the formularies to explain the final conflict between good and evil and a timetable for the end-time. In this view, Revelation is filled with fearsome images of death and destruction: vindictive violence in the name of a final and ultimate justice is unleashed upon a world both fallen and condemned. The righteous who have long endured suffering and persecution will be restored to power; the wicked, and the world in which they have for so long prevailed, will be destroyed; and the creation, begun in such high hope in Genesis, will be brought to an end. All will have good reason for fear and apprehension, for mercy will be in short supply, and the divine justice, long thwarted, finally will obtain.

The early chapters of Revelation are filled with images of a great struggle between the forces of dragons expelled from heaven and the forces of the Lamb. The terrible beast whose symbol is 666 wages war on the faithful, who are required to endure. The struggle is uneven, and appears to favor evil over righteousness. The demonic struggles for possession of the souls of the righteous, a reference to the war in heaven in Revelation 12, are extended into the whole created world.

At chapter 20, John's vision has the battle joined:

Then I saw an angel coming down from heaven, holding in his hand the key to the bottomless pit and a great chain. He seized the dragon, that ancient serpent, who is the Devil and Satan, and bound him for a thousand years, and threw him into the pit, and locked and sealed it over him, so that he would deceive the nations no more, until the thousand years were ended. After that he must be let out for a little while.[6]

During this thousand-year period, those who had not worshiped the beast and who did not bear his mark but had been beheaded, come back to life and reign with Christ. This is what John calls the first resurrection (Revelation 20:5), but at the end of this thousand years, Satan will be released from prison and will come again to deceive the nations and engage in yet another great conflict. Satan and his colleagues surround the saints and the beloved city, but they will not prevail:

And fire came down from heaven and consumed them. And the devil who had deceived them was thrown into the lake of fire and sulfur, where the beast and the false prophets were, and they will be tormented day and night forever and ever.[7]

The vision continues with an image of a great white throne and the dead, both great and small, standing before it awaiting the judgment that will be issued out of the book of life and according to the deeds recorded in it:

Then Death and Hades were thrown into the lake of fire. This is the second death, the lake of fire; and anyone whose name was not found written in the book of life was thrown into the lake of fire.[8]

The conflicts and battles of the first twenty chapters of John's revelation have been the fodder of preachers and artists for two thousand years. The images are compelling and terrifying, and much energy has been consumed in trying to make sense of the symbolic figures, the numbers, and the correspondence of the depicted scenes to historical events. What is often forgotten is that John calls his book a "revelation," or a dream, and while there has long been an art, and even to some a science, in the interpretation of dreams, dreams are not required to conform to the rules of evidence; they constitute neither history nor science. Because of the vivid ambiguity of the visionary images, many in the early church disputed the wisdom of including this particular writing, ascribed to Saint John the Divine, in the canon of scripture, as its capacity for doctrinal edification was not clear.

The character of John's narrative changes at chapter 21, the penultimate chapter, where the author, having disposed of the old conflicts, introduces his famous vision of the new heaven and the new earth. The new Jerusalem comes down from heaven from God, and a new world order is introduced:

> See, the home of God is among mortals. He will dwell with them as their God; they will be his peoples, and God himself will be with them; he will wipe every tear from their eyes. Death will be no more; mourning and crying will be no more, for the first things have passed away.[9]

It has taken twenty chapters and a great deal of violence and struggle to get here, and by this time most readers have been so thoroughly terrified and/or confused that the fact that this vision seems to be the object toward which all the revelation is leading, is lost. It almost seems impossible to believe that Revelation 21 and 22 can bear the burden of all that precedes them.

That, however, is the very salutary point that Barbara Rossing is at pains to make. "Hope," she says, "is surely Revelation's most profound contribution to our world today." John, from the context of despair and hopelessness for the persecuted church, writes of an ultimate hope that says that God has not abandoned his creation and will not destroy his world. Genesis is not repudiated by Revelation, and reconciliation, not vengeance, is the core of the vision with which scripture ends. Rossing writes:

> Revelation is not about an inevitable doomsday for earth, nor about the Rapture. Revelation's story is about seeing the Lamb beside you in every moment of your life. Revelation is about looking more deeply into God's picture and seeing how the Lamb is leading you even now into a world of joy and healing. That is how scripture comes to life for you—not in the Red Horse of the Apocalypse but in the Lamb's river of life, in the tree of life beside the river with its leaves for the healing of the whole world.[10]

Visions of the lake of fire and destruction are trumped by the vision of the new Jerusalem, a world redeemed and restored. The apocalyptic hope is not that we will be rescued from a doomed and fatally flawed creation, but that God's love for the world will result in a renewed beloved community in which what Rossing calls "Lamb power" will prevail over the satanic powers, and the promise of God's incarnation in the world is fulfilled. When one reads the book of Revelation it must always be through the prism of the most famous verse in the Bible, John 3:16:

> For God so loved the world that he gave his only son, so that everyone who believes in him may not perish but may have everlasting life.[11]

In case there is any doubt, John 17 reminds us:

Indeed, God did not send the Son into the world to condemn the world, but in order that the world might be saved through him.[12]

Revelation is not merely a book of terrors, a prediction of dreadful things to come, but a warning and an opportunity. It tells us that we should embrace the vision of a new heaven and a new earth before it is too late. To place the emphasis on the doom and destruction is to fail to take advantage of the opportunity; it is a failure to accept our responsibility to live now, work now, pray now for the coming of the kingdom. Rossing says that Revelation is

a vision of Lamb power in the world. And we are part of that vision. Once we have seen the new creation, the joy of that experience must inform everything that we do.[13]

This is the duty that Walter Russell Bowie captures in his hymn, now too infrequently sung:

O holy city, seen of John,
Where Christ the Lamb doth reign;
Within whose four-square walls shall come
No night, nor need, nor pain.
And where the tears are wiped from eyes
That shall not weep again.

With echoes of a social gospel, Bowie continues:

O shame to us who rest content
While lust and greed for gain
In street and shop and tenement
Wring gold from human pain,

And bitter lips in blind despair cry
"Christ hath died in vain."

Our responsibility for living in the vision and helping to bring it to pass is then made clear:

Give us, O God, the strength to build
The city that hath stood
Too long a dream, whose laws are love,
Whose ways are brotherhood;
And where the sun that shineth is
God's grace for human good.

Our hope consists in helping to realize what God has already willed for the creation he has called good:

Already in the mind of God
That city riseth fair;
Lo, how its splendor challenges
The souls that greatly dare,
Yea, bids us seize the whole of life
And build its glory there.

To read the book of Revelation with courage and not with despair is to find the basis for a reasonable hope and a future worthy of God's promises and our encouraged labors. It is not alone what the text says, or even means, that counts; it is to what the text points that captures our interest. Revelation points to a redeemed, not a doomed future, one in which we have a share. It is the promised time rather than the promised land that now takes precedence, and that is why we call it the gospel, the good news, the gospel of hope.

ELEVEN

Conclusion

My late colleague and friend John Kenneth Galbraith is credited with coining the phrase "the conventional wisdom," by which he meant that which is commonly believed by most people most of the time. He prided himself on living contrary to the conventional wisdom, with remarkably successful results over the course of a long and useful life. There are two bits of conventional wisdom having to do with religion to which I have tried to speak in this book. The first view is that religion is part of the problem and not part of the solution to the human problem, and the second view is that for Christians in particular, the Bible is too tempting a diversion from the hard work of attempting to live a religious life worthy of the times in which we find ourselves.

Those who see religion as the "problem" say that we need only look at the trouble spots of the world, and where there is a problem we will find religion and religious conviction at its heart. The perennial difficulties between Pakistan and India are attributed to the fundamental differences between the devout adherents of Islam and of Hinduism. In the Middle East, trouble is between the Jews and the Muslims. In old Europe it is between the Christians and the Jews, and in Christian countries, trouble is found between and among the varieties of Christian conviction. Apartheid in South Africa enjoyed for years the unqualified support of the Dutch

Reformed church, and slavery and segregation in the United States flourished in the midst of a flourishing Christianity. The pre-seventeenth-century European wars of religion were notorious for their conflicts between Protestants and Catholics, as are the long-standing "troubles" in Northern Ireland.

Not long ago I asked an old student, and a dear friend, how he was finding church life in New York City. I asked him because I knew him in college to be a seriously devout young man, and I knew that he had been church-hunting in New York for some time. He is an intelligent, highly moral, able professional for whom a thinking religion is a serious matter, and who in college had struggled successfully with the great questions of faith: just the sort of person I was proud to have known while he was in college, and I knew that he would be an asset to any congregation in which he finally settled. Thus, I was terribly disappointed when he said that he had gradually given up on church. It was not so much that he found the churches he visited hostile or unfriendly; quite the contrary, they all tried very hard to be the right place and to do the right thing, and they were universally kind and hospitable to him. As a New Yorker who had seen the devastations of September 11th, 2001, too closely, however, he saw religious conviction not simply as inadequate to the needs of modern life, but as a positive danger to it.

He had been reading *The End of Faith* by Sam Harris, and it had rightly disturbed him, for, among other things, Harris says:

Words like "God" and "Allah" must go the way of "Apollo" and "Baal," or they will unmake our world. A few minutes spent wandering the graveyard of bad ideas suggests that such conceptual revolutions are possible. Consider the case of alchemy: it fascinated human beings for over a thousand years, and yet anyone who seriously claims to be a practicing alchemist today will have disqualified himself for most positions of responsibility in our society. Faith-based religion must suffer the same slide into obsolescence.[1]

My young friend had given up on religion, and on the Christian faith in particular, not in anger but in disappointment, and with a profound sense of sadness and loss. He had grown up in a fundamentalist household where it was believed that a literal reading of the Bible provided all that one needed in a fallen and depraved world. When he turned to a more liberal version of the Christian faith, it too proved inadequate to deal with the deep questions confronting a serious, thinking, postmodern American. The fact that flat-earthers and alchemists seemed to be in cultural ascendancy in twenty-first-century America did little to persuade him that religious conviction made any positive contribution to life as he felt obliged to live it.

Another young friend, blessed or cursed with an active social conscience—one of those admirable young people determined to do as much good as he can when he finds himself in the middle of social problems that admit of no simple solutions—is convinced that government is part of the problem and not part of the solution, because the prevailing political philosophy lacks the will to invest itself in the solutions to social dilemmas. Conventionally religious, he asks why it is that the church is always the social and moral caboose and never the engine that drives the train for good. Most churches long ago abandoned a social gospel in favor of a private piety of personal salvation; the churches avoided the AIDS pandemic until the secular world shamed them into paying some attention; and so-called peace churches are still a minority, considered by their mainstream colleagues as peculiar, even dangerous. The only issues that seem to fire the imaginations of most churches are abortion, homosexuality, the evils of evolution, and the anticipated end of the world. Surely, he adds, communities of faith can and ought to do better than this.

For many, and, alas, among many whom I count as friends, the conventional wisdom is that religion has run its course and is no longer a constructive part of the conversation concerning the future well-being of human society. When the European Union was attempting to draft a document that would define its cultural heritage and serve as a basis for future constructive action, religion in general was found to be too divisive; and the Christian inheritance, once the glory of European civilization and whose monuments punctuate nearly every landscape, was regarded with near embarrassment, the entreaties and examples of the pope and the Vatican notwithstanding.

For others, the conventional wisdom is the perennial call "back to the Bible," usually the first line of defense against what Pope Pius X, at the beginning of the twentieth century, called the acids of modernity. The so-called battles for the Bible in the first half of the twentieth century were fought between those who saw the Bible as a bulwark against the destabilizing forces of modernity and who therefore rejected biblical criticism as destructive of biblical authority and a concession to the false claims of modern science, and those who felt that the only way the Bible could be rescued for modern times was to use the tools that modernity provided to prove that the Bible was still relevant and useful. So-called modernists, who took this point of view, and the equally inadequately named fundamentalists, who took the opposite view, fought with each other for the right to possess the iconic book, the Bible, as their key to understanding and, to no small degree, controlling the modern world.

In his famous sermon "Shall the Fundamentalists Win?" New York's Harry Emerson Fosdick argued that this battle was diverting the churches from more important work and, at the same time, alienating the young on whom the future welfare of the churches and the world depended. When he gave his sermon, which through the support of John D. Rockefeller, Jr., became perhaps the most widely read sermon in America in 1923, he concluded that the answer to "Shall the Fundamentalists Win?" was a resounding "No!" So it might have seemed, but he was wrong. The fundamentalist position, embraced by many but not all evangelicals, is now mainstream not only in Christian America but increasingly around the world. The conventional wisdom is that this is now the way religion is done.

I began my career as a preacher and teacher at Harvard in 1970, and since 1974, I have had charge of the University's chapel, The Memorial Church. In all these years I have found myself between two significant encampments in the place that many persist in calling Godless Harvard. Nathan Marsh Pusey, president of Harvard from 1953 to 1971, once characterized these encampments as "those who believe too little" and "those who believe too much." Those who believe too little, from the Christian point of view, are those who believe that the secular, scientific, and increasingly pluralistic university now belongs to them. It is not that they are active opponents of religion: religion is too minor and parochial a matter to concern them now, anachronistic, at best a harmless vestige of an earlier age. They are even vaguely tolerant of religion as long as it does not get in the way or, as one colleague said, "frighten the horses."

Those whom Mr. Pusey characterized as believing too much tend to see the modern university as a place inimical to faith and hostile to the practice of religion. Hence, only the full wealth of conviction will do in the fight against the rival and false religion of secular humanism and the hegemony of science. Many of those people appropriate a concept once popular in Harvard's seventeenth-century Puritan past: they see themselves as the *Militia Christi*, the Army of Christ, prepared to defend the faithful against the threats of the classroom and the academic culture. Under their auspices, Bible studies and discipleship groups flourish.

The practitioners of religion are many and, to be fair, not all of them "believe too much." As a result of Harvard's self-conscious efforts at diversity, persons from many religious traditions other than those of the Christian West have come to the university, and have brought with them the practices of their own religious traditions. Just as America itself has become more visibly diverse in the practices of religion, so too has Harvard. Muslim, Hindu, and Buddhist students, to name but a few of the great traditions previously rare or unknown at Harvard, are now well represented here, and their numbers are increasing. One can argue that there is more practice of religion at Harvard now than probably at any point in the last century.

Over the years I have found myself dealing increasingly with a group of people who cannot be said to belong to either of Mr. Pusey's categories of too much or too little belief. College is often the place where people discover religion and come to faith for the first time, and more and more of our students come from truly secular homes, homes in which their parents, the products of the first fully secular generation, keep no religious traditions. A student discovers religious ideas in an English course, sees the representation of religious figures in a fine arts course or a museum, sings sacred music in one of the many choruses and wonders what the text means, and sometimes even takes religion courses in an effort to understand the "other" and to make meaning for him- or herself. Many of them wander into The Memorial Church, and there they encounter preaching, teaching, worship, and music, and a community of people who have not left their heads at the door and yet are interested in all those things. These are people for whom the "old, old story" is quite new and challenging. One clever young fellow, who heard in church the lesson on the Prodigal Son from the Gospel of John for the first time, was curious, and asked me if I could tell him more about the story.

For readers from all traditions, including those who are just discovering the Christian faith or are discouraged by their experience of it, I have written this book. As I am at pains to point out, the Bible is not the end of the Christian faith; rather, it is the point of departure, and I am convinced that it offers more good news than bad, and points away from itself to what is called the gospel. Jesus, after all, did not become incarnate in the world as a great Bible teacher; he came to proclaim the glad tidings, to preach the gospel. Seeing where that takes us is what I mean when I suggest that we are meant to go beyond the Bible in order to discover the gospel, and sometimes that means becoming reacquainted with things we once knew and perhaps have forgotten. In other cases, it involves a brave new adventure beyond the conventional wisdom and our own comfort zones. To take this on seriously requires intellectual and spiritual courage, and that is why I am persuaded that we are ready—some for the first time, and some again—to hear what the great theologian Paul Tillich has to say about living in dangerous and difficult times without loss of hope or integrity.

When I was an undergraduate at Bates College, which I entered in 1961, Paul Tillich was the theologian of culture, known not just to the divinity students but to every reasonably well read person in America. He was ubiquitous as a lecturer and preacher on college campuses, his books were on nearly every reading list, and his face appeared on the cover of *Time* magazine. He was not an easy person nor was he one seeking popularity, and he did not choose to compete with television's Bishop Fulton J. Sheen or the enormously successful Norman Vincent Peale. He did not fill stadiums around the world as did the charismatic Billy Graham with his crusades, and thus Tillich's popularity was all the more unusual and noteworthy, in large part because he took the fact of existential despair seriously and realized that beneath the façade of a vibrant public religiosity there hid a nagging, dissipating suspicion that somehow meaning and purpose were, if not lost, then severely compromised. The conventional wisdom was that few would bother to read the works of a German theologian who did not share in the usual optimistic pieties or know the concept of "dumbing down."

Tillich taught at Harvard and was gone by the time I arrived, but one of the first public events I remember attending in The Memorial Church was his memorial service, held in the fall of 1965. Professor Tillich had already attained a form of intellectual immortality in his most popular and enduring book, *The Courage to Be*; he accepted the realities of a world that could never be reconstructed in its old form with all of its cozy assumptions and presuppositions intact. Humpty Dumpty had fallen, and despite the best efforts of liberals and conservatives, modernists and fundamentalists, could not be put back together again: the "courage to be" was the courage to live in such a world without despair. Courage, as Tillich knew, did not overcome fear and was not the opposite of fear; it was how one faced the reality of fear and moved through and beyond it. In his lectures, books, and sermons he addressed himself to what he called "the anxiety of meaninglessness," and he wrote of "the attempt to take this anxiety into the courage to be as oneself."[2]

For Paul Tillich, the courage to be is "the courage to accept oneself as accepted in spite of being unacceptable." While the book *The Courage to Be* may have been rough going for many looking for a quick and effortless inspirational read, the sermons he preached on college campuses all across the country were much more accessible. Perhaps his most famous sermon, "You Are Accepted," gives us the essence of what he meant to say, and even after fifty years it says what we need to hear today:

You are accepted. You are accepted, accepted by that which is greater than you, and the name of which you do not know. Do not ask for the name now; perhaps you will find it later. Do not try to do anything now; perhaps later you will do much. Do not seek for anything; do not intend anything. Simply accept the fact that you are accepted. If that happens to us, we experience grace.[3]

The popular magazines that market themselves by ranking American colleges have introduced us all to a category by which college popularity is examined. Called the acceptance rate, it does not refer to the number of persons a college accepts, but rather to the number of persons who accept the acceptance of their college. Those colleges achieving high ratings have the highest number of people actually accepting their acceptances, and it is these that comprise a college's entering class. It is a happy situation when the college that wants you is the college you want to attend, and do.

Tillich argues that accepting the fact that God has accepted us, even if in our heart of hearts we find ourselves unacceptable, is the first act of courage that allows us to cope with an inhospitable world. God is more generous than we are, and to realize and accept that is to know what grace is. It means that we can begin not as exiles, aliens, or the condemned, but as people who have, through no merit of our own, found favor in God's eyes. Armed with the courage of God's convictions about ourselves, we are not only accepted but enabled and empowered; and that discovery, the conventional wisdom notwithstanding, allows us to live and work and even die in a world not of despair and fear and terror but of promise and hope.

It is one thing to accept oneself and, Professor Tillich notwithstanding, that may be very easy to do, "just as I am, without one plea," to quote Charlotte Elliott's well-known hymn; but in order to take the good news as seriously and as joyously as we should, we ought to accept what is available to us in a better understanding of who Jesus is and what it is that he teaches. In the reading, thinking, and praying that has led to this book I am convinced of two things, neither of which is novel but both of which are essential. First, what we know of God or about God we know because of what we know about Jesus; and second, Jesus' proclamation is meant to take us from a world that is to a world that is to be. This means that while we are not to be obsessed with the so-called historical Jesus, we have to take seriously what Jesus requires of those who would hear and follow him. It further means that while history and precedent are important, the only place toward which faithful Christians are to look, and the only place in which there is real promise for the good news, is the future.

When Jesus came preaching, it was to disturb the status quo. From this we must learn that God is not to be propitiated either with things as they are or with things as they have been, and for those who, like me, take tradition seriously, this is hard news to take. All of us imagine that somewhere in the past there once existed a community of faith, a corpus of belief more pleasing to God than what is presently on offer, and as a historian I have spent much of my life searching the past for just such things. There is an appeal to the so-called primitive church, and I understand the call for a "biblical" faith and the essentially conservative nature of Christian belief and practice. Somehow we have been persuaded that the nearer we are to the days of the Lord and the earliest believers, the more faithful we are, and one of the strongest appeals of the Roman Catholic church, especially to those of us who are not Roman Catholic, is its sense of continuity and antiquity. There are many Protestant communities that work hard to emulate the first communities of belief and practice in the mistaken view that those communities were somehow nearer the truth, and that thus for us to be near the truth we should be as much like them as possible.

Yet, if we read what Jesus says and see what he has done, we must be convinced that the status quo, ancient or contemporary, is still not where he would have us be. The notion that we should invest in some sense of primitive purity rather than in the adventure of what is not yet and is yet to come suggests that we really do not trust the nature of Jesus' ministry, and that should he come again as he came before, we would disregard him in the same way. What is it that persuades us that God prefers history to prophecy, that the past is somehow safer and thus more sacred than the future?

A social activist once asked me a sincere question whose assumptions are difficult to refute: "Why is the church always last in any movement for reform or change?" It is easy to refer to the Roman Catholic church's unwillingness to take the science of Galileo seriously until well into the twentieth century, and to the reactionary instincts of such popes as Pius IX and X, for whom everything since Thomas Aquinas's time was a curse of modernity. Then there are the cases where much of Protestantism resists the course of the modern age and responds only with hostility or indifference to secular claims for change. Although the Quakers were ahead on the subject of the abolition of slavery, the vast majority of American Protestants resisted any change in the American racial status quo, and the Southern Baptists did not repent of their complicity in slavery and segregation until the closing third of the twentieth century. Even today the Roman Catholic church resists the ordination of women despite the radical inclusion of women in Jesus' discourse, and most, if not all, changes for social justice take their leads from the secular world.

The emotional appeal of the "old-time religions" as "good enough for me" may confirm us in the habits of our ancestors, but it does little to take us into that terra incognita, that unknown land of challenge and opportunity, where Jesus would lead us. We would do well to remember Paul's words to the Philippians:

...one thing I do, forgetting what lies behind and straining forward to what lies ahead, I press on toward the goal for the prize of the upward call of God in Christ Jesus.[4]

Lest we forget that this is how the thoughtful and faithful should proceed, Paul continues:

Let those of us who are mature be thus minded.[5]

I once preached a sermon on why God should love us if we did not love what God loves, in which I argued that by the example of Jesus and the words of the prophets, God loves the marginalized, the outcast, and the questionable in society—the very people whom we, as a rule, keep out of our churches and out of positions of leadership. It is fashionable to help the poor but not to empower them, and until recently, for many Christians it was acceptable to confine the spiritual gifts of women to a lesser order of magnitude within the church. Today it remains acceptable among far too many Christians to regard homosexuals as beyond the pale of the church unless, while remaining homosexual, they cease to behave as such. For certain Anglican prelates, including the archbishop of Nigeria, Peter Akinola, to argue that they are defending the faith by excluding the homosexual faithful on biblical grounds represents a degree of hubris, ignorance, and noncharity that baffles the mind. Their future is likely to be disconcerting, if not downright unpleasant.

For those people of God, however, who represent the view that God is the future and that the time to come is the most compelling of all times, the good news speaks of a time that has not yet been but is to be. These are the people for whom the book of Revelation is not a book of revenge but a book of vision and reconciliation between a fallen and a restored creation. What was disturbing about

Jesus was that he could see that, and proclaimed it to the establishment of his day. When it is written in the account of the wise men's visit to King Herod in their search for the infant king that "Herod was troubled and all Jerusalem with him," the suggestion is that the very existence of Jesus, before he had uttered a word or done a deed, was a threat to things as they were and had been. Nothing now, including Herod and all Jerusalem, was safe from change and transformation, and thus has it ever been.

Jesus faced that future in hope, and so too did the early church; and every time the faithful pray, in the words ascribed to Jesus, "Thy kingdom come, thy will be done on earth as it is in heaven…" we invoke a confidence in the coming good news not only in heaven but right here on earth. At no point does Jesus make the past sacred. Never does he point to an age that was superior to the age that is or is to come, and yet so many of us take pride in our fidelity to the age that is past, pledging our fealty to Nicea, Chalcedon, or Westminster, as if theirs were the last moments in which the Spirit spoke. Jesus never appealed to some past theological consensus; he claimed the future for God, and for those people of God who were prepared to regard the future as the place where God would perform his transforming wonders.

Some say that such a view yields to a naïve hope that tomorrow will be better than today when the sober record of history says just the opposite. Thus, like a drowning man, we hold onto the wreckage of a past security, terrified that if we let go we will perish. The past gives us encouraging examples, but only enough to enable us to persevere into the future. As a Christian I believe that our best days are ahead of us, and by this I do not mean that the ecclesiastical establishment as we have known it will rise again and rule the world, for not only is that not likely to happen, but I certainly hope that it doesn't. What I do mean is that only in the time to come will we have an opportunity to see what it is that God has in store for us, only in the time to come will we understand what it means to pray for the coming of the kingdom. The future as proclaimed in the good news is not something to fear: we should not cower in spiritual bomb shelters as otherwise sensible Americans hid in bomb shelters in the 1950s in anticipation of nuclear war. Rather, I think we must make the hymn/prayer of The Reverend Frederick L. Hosmer our own, and our hope not mere nostalgia for what never was, but an earnest expectation of what is to be, whose signs are among us even here, even now.

> *Thy kingdom come! on bended knee the passing ages pray;*
> *And faithful souls have yearned to see on earth that kingdom's*
> *　　day.*
> *But the slow watches of the night not less to God belong,*
> *And for the everlasting right the silent stars are strong.*
> *And lo, already on the hills the flags of dawn appear;*
> *Gird up your loins, ye prophet souls, proclaim the day is near.*
> *The day in whose clear shining light all wrong shall stand*
> *　　revealed,*
> *When justice shall be throned in might, and every hurt be*
> *　　healed;*
> *When knowledge, hand in hand with peace, shall walk the*
> *　　earth abroad;*
> *The day of perfect righteousness, the promised day of God.*[6]

Life in such a world is neither dreary nor fearful. God's love, present at our creation, will also sustain our redemption, and to be redeemed is to become what God has always intended us to be. We are accepted, as Paul Tillich noted, but it is our joyful task to accept what God has proposed for us, a future in which promise and fulfillment meet. To that end we live and work and pray, and that is good news for those who dare to hear it. Nothing less than this confidence in God's future and ours is what Jesus means when he said:

I am come that they might have life, and that they might have it more abundantly.[7]

The future is God's, it is ours, it is good; and that is good news.

Acknowledgments

In the writing of a book there are many obligations to acknowledge. My first is to my publishers, and in particular to Roger M. Freet, whose generous patience and timely encouragement made bearable the burden of writing, long delayed, and caused me to look forward to the completion of this project. I thank also my agent, John Taylor Williams, who more often than is his wont waited quietly and patiently for me to do the right thing; no author could ask for a better guide through the wilderness of writing. I thank my colleagues on the staff of The Memorial Church, especially my executive assistant, Janetta Cothran Randolph, who encouraged me by gestures great and small to finish what I had begun. Finally, as in every written project from my hand, the hand and mind and heart of Cynthia Wight Rossano are at the center of this enterprise. I thank her for her encouragement, for editing and preparing the manuscript, and for her assistance at every level of idea and execution. There would be no book without her.

Every academic author owes a debt of gratitude to the students whom to teach is a joy, and most of mine will not realize how helpful they have been in the forging of ideas. I thank them, one and all. A preacher is also indebted to a congregation, and I am particularly indebted to the congregation of The Memorial Church where, over long years, many of these ideas were first hatched and heard. I thank the people of my congregation for their confidence, and for the joy of service as their pastor.

Finally, I dedicate this book to old friends, Pelham and Sterly Wilder, of Duke University. I have been a friend of Duke University for many years, and when Pelham and Sterly endowed a preachership at Duke Chapel, I was appointed its first incumbent. Each year when I am invited to preach at Duke, I do so under the auspices of the Wilder name.

Pelham Wilder received his Ph.D. in chemistry in 1949 from Harvard. He served as Professor of Pharmacology in The Duke University School of Medicine from 1977 to 2000, and from 1949 as University Distinguished Service Professor of Chemistry, now emeritus. From 1977 to 2000 he also served as University Marshal and Chief of Protocol, where he had charge of Duke's public ceremonies, including Baccalaureate and Commencement. When he entered Duke Chapel, or any other place in his official capacity with the great mace of office on his shoulder, he was rightly described by admirers as a "procession of one." Not only was Pelham obsessed with details, as befits a chief of protocol, but he also understood the big picture and regarded ceremonial, well conducted, as maintaining Duke's rightful place in the ancient academic inheritance. It was always reassuring to me to see the Wilders in their customary places among the throngs in Duke Chapel, and now, even in his retirement and widowerhood, Pelham Wilder sustains a lively interest in all that matters to his university and chapel. I count his friendship among my chief treasures, and I offer this book as a small tribute to him and his late wife, whose hospitality of hearth and heart has always been most gracious and generous. Such friendships are rare.

PJG
Oceanside
Plymouth, Massachusetts
January 2007

Notes

INTRODUCTION

1. In Edward Farley, *Practicing Gospel: Unconventional Thoughts on the Church's Ministry* (Louisville, KY: Westminster John Knox Press, 2003).
2. Judges 21:25.

CHAPTER 1: *We Start with the Bible*

1. Unless otherwise noted, biblical citations are from the King James Version, the Revised Standard Version, or the New Revised Standard Version.

CHAPTER 2: *An Offending Gospel*

1. Matthew 3:2–3.
2. Matthew 11:3.
3. Matthew 11:4–6.
4. Matthew 4:8.
5. Paraphrase of Matthew 27:39.
6. Samuel Johnson, 1846.
7. Matthew 20:15–16.

CHAPTER 3: *The Risks of Nonconformity*

1. Hebrews 11:37.
2. "The Triumph of the Authoritarians," *The Boston Globe*, July 14, 2006.

CHAPTER 4: *What Would Jesus Have Me Do?*

1. Matthew 6:33.
2. Matthew 22:37.
3. Matthew 22:37–40.
4. Luke 10:25–37.
5. Arland J. Hultgren, *The Parables of Jesus* (Grand Rapids: Eerdmans, 2000), 95.

CHAPTER 5: *The Gospel and Fear*

1. John 16:33.
2. Ecclesiasticus 2:2.
3. Romans 8:38–39.

4. Hugh Martin, *The Beatitudes* (New York: Harper & Bros., 1953).

CHAPTER 6: *The Gospel and Conflict*

1. Graham Ferguson Lacey, ed., *My Favourite Hymn* (London: Robson Books, 1999).
2. Revelation 21:1–5, *Good News for Modern Man.*
3. 1 Timothy 6:12.
4. See *The New York Times*, August 2, 2006, p. A23.
5. Reinhold Niebuhr, "Christianity and Power Politics," in *The Treasury of Religious and Spiritual Quotations: Words to Live By*, edited by Rebecca Davis and Susan Mesner (Pleasantville, NY: Reader's Digest Association/Stonesong Press, 1994).

CHAPTER 7: *The Gospel and the Future*

1. 2 Thessalonians 2:1–3.
2. T. S. Eliot, "Journey of the Magi."
3. 1 Corinthians 2:9.
4. Revelation 22:3–5.
5. Matthew 20:15–16.
6. Micah 7:18, NEB.
7. Jonah 4:1–3, REB.

CHAPTER 8: *A Social Gospel*

1. Richard Land, *Real Homeland Security: The America God Will Bless* (Nashville: Broadman & Holman, 2004), 177.
2. Linda Seger, *Jesus Rode a Donkey: Why Republicans Don't Have the Corner on Christ* (Cincinnati: Adams Media, 2006), 39.
3. Seger, *Jesus Rode a Donkey*, 48.
4. Seger, *Jesus Rode a Donkey*, 48.

CHAPTER 9: *An Inclusive Gospel*

1. Helen Lemmel (1863–1961), 1922.
2. Galatians 3:1–3, REB.
3. H. Darrell Lance, in *The InSpiriter*, Summer 2006, 10.
4. Galatians 5:6, REB.
5. Jeffrey S. Siker, in *The Covenant Connection*, Summer 2006, 3.
6. Siker, 4.
7. Siker, 4.
8. *Harvard Divinity Today* 2 (Summer 2006): 6.
9. *Harvard Divinity Today* 2 (Summer 2006): 6.

CHAPTER 10: *A Gospel of Hope*

1. Halford E. Luccock, *Living Without Gloves* (New York: Oxford, 1957).
2. Emily Dickinson (1830–1886); from *The Complete Poems* (1955), no. 254; cited in *The Treasury of Religious and Spiritual Quotations* (Reader's Digest, 1994), 235.

3. Romans 5:1–5.
4. Romans 5:3–5.
5. Barbara R. Rossing; *The Rapture Exposed: The Message of Hope in the Book of Revelation* (New York: Basic Books, 2004), 120.
6. Revelation 20:1–3.
7. Revelation 20:9–10.
8. Revelation 20:14–15.
9. Revelation 21:3–4.
10. Rossing, *The Rapture Exposed*, 171.
11. John 3:16.
12. John 3:17.
13. Rossing, *The Rapture Exposed*, 165.

CHAPTER 11: *Conclusion*

1. Sam Harris, *The End of Faith: Religion, Terror, and the Future of Reason* (New York: Norton, 2005), 14.
2. Cited in Gomes, Introduction to Paul Tillich's *The Courage to Be*, 2d ed. (New Haven: Yale Univ. Press, 2000), xx.
3. Gomes, Introduction, xxii.
4. Philippians 3:13–14.
5. Philippians 3:15.
6. Frederick Lucian Hosmer, 1891.
7. John 10:10.

Index

Page numbers of Bible chapters and verses appear in bold print.